Basketball's High-Powered Multiflex Offense

Bob Peterson

Parker Publishing Company
West Nyack, New York

© 1986 by

PARKER PUBLISHING COMPANY, INC.

West Nyack, N.Y.

Library of Congress Cataloging-in-Publication Data

Peterson, Robert G.
  Basketball's high-powered multiflex offense.

  Includes index.
  1. Basketball—Offense. 2. Basketball—Coaching.
I. Title.
GV889.P48 1986   796.32'32   85-30966

ISBN 0-13-069220-4

Printed in the United States of America

Preface

Bob Peterson and basketball are bound together in this coaching book just as they are each and every single day throughout the year. Bob has a burning desire to make his mark as a basketball coach and it's been a lifelong dream to present *Basketball's High-Powered Multiflex Offense* so others can benefit from his dedication and hard work. He's attended clinics, made voluminous notes, charted games, and discussed basketball with anyone and everyone he thought could help him develop "his" style of play. The result is an offensive system that can be used against virtually any type of defense whether it be man, zone, match-ups, or combination defenses.

Bob Peterson is different from most aspiring coaches who dream about coaching success. He did something about it. He hustled at the game until he got a coaching job and, once on his way, he didn't talk about bad situations or losing seasons. Years of hard work and planning went into his apprenticeship and many young athletes have benefited as a result.

Today, Bob Peterson is a poised, outspoken, confident master of the game he loves. He believes in himself, his players, and in his style of play. Nothing is as important to him as basketball and the impact the game has on his athletes. He is patient and popular with his players, who respect him as a leader and admire him as a friend. His successes have left him completely unchanged.

You will find all the details in this book—a comprehensive offensive system designed to free players for excellent percentage shots. This book contains all the information vital to coaching success. Don't miss it!

Bob Voight
Assistant Basketball Coach
Marquette University

Why the Multiflex Offense?

The Multiflex Offense is a high-powered offense that works equally well against man-to-man and zone defenses. This eliminates the need for multiple offenses. Many coaches will have two or more offenses for man-to-man defenses, another for even-front zones, still another for odd-front zones, and yet another for match-up zones. On top of this they will put in the fast break, one or two different press offenses, maybe a third press offense if the ball is taken out of bounds on the side of the backcourt, and a fourth press offense to beat half-court traps. These coaches need still another offense to speed up the tempo, another to slow it down, and finally, another offense to counter combination defenses. Players are expected to learn up to 12 different offenses and, at the same time, they must learn to recognize the defense before they can determine which of these offenses they are to use. By using the Multiflex Offense, a team is ready to go against every defense ever used in basketball.

In having just one offense a team will learn the offense considerably better, with less time needed to perfect it; there is considerably less confusion, especially in crucial situations; and most important, the team will develop strong confidence in its ability to score in all situations and against all opponents.

This book was written to help coaches who feel the same frustrations I have in not being able to score against the good defensive teams, the ones who seem to take away everything you want to do. This offense, when run properly, will free players against even the best defensive team you will face.

The Multiflex Offense has a number of steps to it; they follow simply and logically, and can be taught to basketball players of all ages. It involves some of the basic aspects of offensive basketball, yet puts them in a framework that will allow your players to get free every time down the court.

In searching for an offense that would be effective against zone defenses we came upon the idea of using our man-to-man offense. By using the same rules that we have for reading the defensive adjustments in the man-to-man, we found the Multiflex Offense was the most effective offense we ever had for zones.

The offense can be used on all levels—grade school through college. The extent to which you develop the offense will depend on the experience and ability level of your players. It is a simple offense that takes advantage of any defensive adjustments your team may see.

The best part of the Multiflex Offense is its adaptability to your personnel. You can use your best five players, whether that's the traditional two guards, two forwards, and a center, or all five guards. The only position that is truly necessary is a good point guard. If you don't have a good point guard in any offense you're in for a long season!

The offense is limited only to what you hold as your personal philosophy. It is easy to adapt this to any fastbreak style and yet it can be used in a slow-down style of play. In fact, you can go so far as to use this offense as your delay or stall game.

The offense was initially designed to counter the pressure of man-to-man defense and has evolved into an offense for all purposes, thus the name "Multiflex Offense."

As with anything new it may take a week or two of adjusting to the moves, cuts, and reads, but once the players have become acquainted with it they will be a much more efficient offensive machine.

The Multiflex goes beyond the current offensive trends because it not only gives the players a certain amount of freedom, but has the added advantage of being able to go to set plays whenever the situation dictates. By using this offense, long scoring droughts are highly unlikely. This means a more consistent and better scoring offense for your team. A special note for you as the coach: You can make this offense as complex or as simple as you want. This depends on the age level and experience of your players.

Finally, the Multiflex is enjoyable. Fans love it, players find it very exciting, and you will find it to be the best offense you have ever coached. The only people who won't like it will be your opponents.

Contents

Diagram Keys

Offensive players	1,2,3,4,5
Player with the ball	①
Player Options	1
Player cuts	⟶
Straight pass	- - - - ▸
Bounce Pass	
Lob Pass	
Screens	⊢———
Player dribbling	∿∿∿
Man-to-man defender	×2 or 2×
Zone defender	×
Shot	
Rebound	⬏
Steal	S

1

Basic Sets and Cuts of the Multiflex Offense

POSITIONING

The basic Multiflex Offense starts with a 1–4 alignment, using two posts, two wings, and a point guard. The point guard, who should be your best ball handler and passer, is out in front above the top of the key. The two wings start about eight feet out from the lane and even with the third lane marker. The posts begin about a step lower than the wings facing out away from the basket (Diagram 1-1). We have found it best to number each of the positions. In a traditional lineup, (1) would be the ball-handling guard, (2) would be the off or

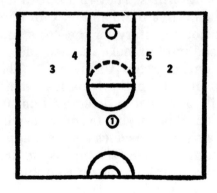

Diagram 1-1

shooting guard, (3) the small forward, (4) the power forward, and (5) the center. In the Multiflex Offense it is not necessary to stick with these positions. You can use any combination of players at the different positions, depending on the relative strength of your personnel. At times we have used as many as four guards at once with the fifth person as small forward. We have also used three centers and a power forward along with a point guard and not had to vary the offense. It is totally flexible and easily adaptable to all players.

CUTS AND SCREENS

The offense starts with the wings exchanging sides. The key to their moving is in the position of the point guard. As the point drives his man down inside the top of the circle, the wings should be about halfway across the lane. The timing of this is extremely important. Usually the wings will start to cross as the point guard moves into the front court. The exact timing will depend on your players. The wing on the left (facing the basket) always sets the pick for the wing on the right. The left wing must headhunt and find the right wing's defensive man, then go and screen him. The right wing [(2) in Diagram 1-2] must always cut baseline around everyone (Diagram 1-2). This ensures that the defensive wings will have to fight through two or more picks to stay with their men.

As the wings are cutting across the lane, the posts are also setting picks for the wings. They first screen the nearside defensive wing, then turn around and look for the offside defensive wing. It is not necessary for the posts actually to make contact; they need only to make the defenders change direction, even if it's only one step (Diagram 1-3). The posts should take a half step into the path of the man they are trying to screen. This will prevent the defender from taking a direct path across the lane when trying to cover the wing. It is important that the posts set themselves soon enough so they won't be called for setting a moving screen. As the first wing moves past them, the posts turn and again step into the path of the second defensive wing, who has come across the lane with the far wing (Diagram 1-4).

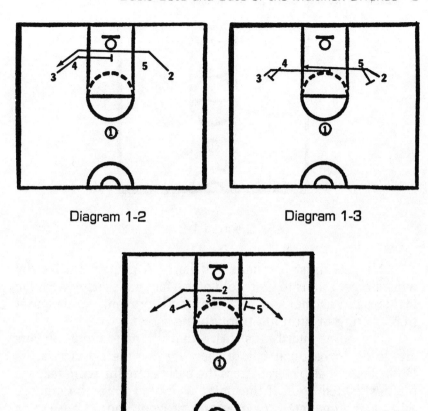

Diagram 1-2   Diagram 1-3

Diagram 1-4

The point guard drives his man down to just inside the top of the key. This will give the correct spacing for the point guard to be able to make a sharp, crisp pass to either side.

Coaching Point: The point guard must stay in the free throw lane extended so as not to commit to one side or the other (Diagram 1-5). Keeping the ball in the middle of the court forces the defense to play honestly. If the ball is brought down one side, the defense can declare a side and overplay the offense on that side while sagging in to help out from the other.

Also, it is very important that the point guard keep his head on the basket, so that he can see both sides of the court equally well.

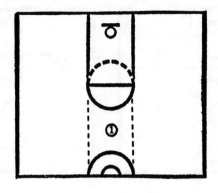

Diagram 1-5

All cuts must be sharp and hard. A good habit for the wings to get into is to grab hold of the far post's jersey with the inside hand as they cut past. This will prevent the defender from cutting or jumping through the screen.

The point guard must learn to anticipate which players are going to be open before they get completely across the lane. He must also start to pass the ball before the wing reaches his designated spot. If the point waits too long, the defense will have a chance to recover and prevent your offense from starting where you want.

Passing to the Wing

As the wing receives the ball he should catch it in the shooting position and square to the basket, pivoting forward on the outside foot (the foot away from the baseline). Pivoting this way has two main advantages. First, this makes for better offensive balance and positioning by putting a little distance between the wing and the post. This will make it more difficult for the defensive wing to sag in and help on the post if the ball is passed inside. Second, this will ensure that the wing can make his crossover move to the baseline if he needs to beat the defensive pressure. The strongside post [(5) in Diagram 1-6], the one on the side of the ball, pivots open to the ball. How he pivots is determined by the positioning of the defender covering him. This will be discussed in chapter 3. The

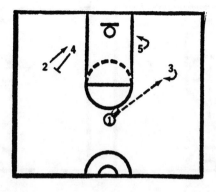

Diagram 1-6

weakside post again steps into the defensive path of the weakside wing's defender, forcing this man to either go above or below the screen as the wing begins to make his cut to the basket (Diagram 1-6).

The point guard hesitates or fakes, then cuts down the lane looking for a return pass from the wing. The weakside wing cuts toward the basket and through the screen of the near post. As his defensive man goes around the screen, the wing will read the defender's position and make a cut based on this. This situation will be covered in greater detail in Chapter 3. For now assume that the defensive man will protect the basket, and that tells the wing [(2) in Diagram 1-7] to break out to the middle of the free throw line, after taking his man toward the basket one or two steps. As he gets to the free throw line he should get himself in a position for a pass from the strongside wing (Diagram 1-7). If the pass is thrown the wing must try to get behind it, catching it so that he will be in a position to go up immediately with the ball for a shot. Being "behind the ball" means catching the ball in a shooting position and facing the basket. This will prevent the defender from recovering to his man before he can get the shot off.

The point guard has cut down the middle looking for a return pass from the wing. As he reaches the broken circle, he now cuts to the weak side in front of the weakside defensive wing. When he is directly in front of the defender we want the point to use a hesitation or stutter step, but he should keep

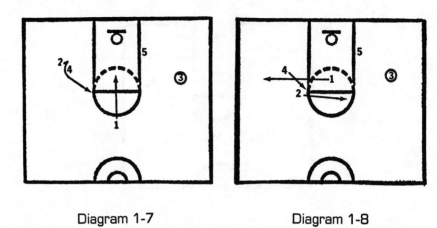

Diagram 1-7   Diagram 1-8

moving. The point guard will end up in a position directly across from the wing with the ball (Diagram 1-8).

The strongside post stays above the box as he posts. This keeps him in a position to use the backboard when he turns baseline. If he allows himself to get any deeper than this, he will not only have trouble using the board, he may actually find himself behind it, unable to get a shot off at all. The actual body positioning of anyone posting up will also be covered in Chapter 3 (Diagram 1-9).

If the post doesn't receive a pass by the count of two, he makes a diagonal cut toward the opposite corner of the free throw line. As he does this, the weakside post [(4) in Diagram 1-10], who has moved up the lane after setting a pick for the wing, cuts across the lane to the ball. The weakside post has the option of cutting either high or low. If he cuts low he will cut behind the strongside post and post up just above the box. The screening post rolls open to the ball moving to the high-post area (Diagram 1-10).

Using the Weakside Post's Screen

If the weakside post comes across the lane high, he should continue out to the wing and set a screen for the strongside wing (Diagram 1-11).

If the strongside post doesn't receive a pass he must now clear to the weak side. The weakside post [(4) in Diagram 1-11]

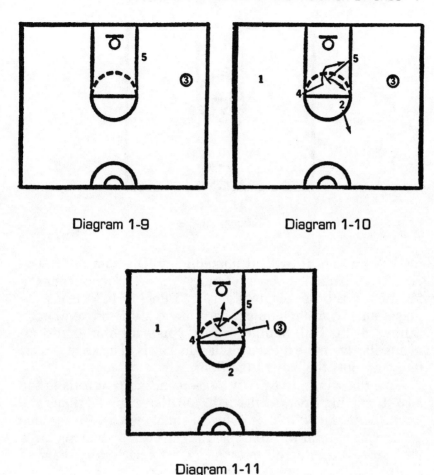

Diagram 1-9

Diagram 1-10

Diagram 1-11

always sets the screen on the topside of the wing. The wing has the option of either using the screen or driving the baseline. If he uses the screen he will drive to the near corner of the free throw line. He should use a jab-step move to beat his man and he should get to the elbow (the corner of the free throw line) in no more than two dribbles. The weakside wing [(2) in Diagram 1-12], who is now on the point, and the point guard again exchange. They should move as soon as the wing puts the ball on the floor. The player coming from the point, in this case the wing, will always set the screen for the player coming from the wing, in this case the point. This player should come off the screen looking for a possible pass from the opposite wing. He should try to get into a position where he can catch

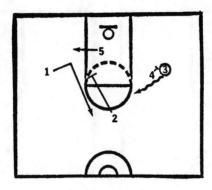

Diagram 1-12

the ball and go up with it immediately (Diagram 1-12). The post away from the screen "ducks" into the lane from the low-post position (Diagram 1-13). "Ducking In" means the player should make a quick, hard move to the broken circle, calling for the ball. In other words, you want him to post up momentarily on the broken circle. His key is to make the cut as the wing puts the ball on the floor.

As the wing drives past the screen, the post rolls to the basket, staying open to the ball. On the second dribble the wing should know if he is going to shoot or pass. His options are: the post (4) rolling to the basket, the post (5) ducking in, or the point (1) coming off the screen on the weakside (Diagram 1-14).

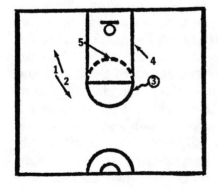 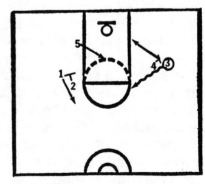

Diagram 1-13   Diagram 1-14

Moving Away from the Screen

If the wing [(3) in Diagram 1-15] doesn't use the screen, he should make a crossover move to the baseline. He should need only one hard dribble (power dribble) to get to the basket. As before, the opposite post ducks in while the screening post rolls. This time the screener rolls to the corner of the free throw line. The point guard now screens for the wing, who continues past the screen to the weakside corner. The point guard moves out on top for defensive balance (Diagram 1-15).

If nothing is open, neither the post going to the low-post position nor off the screen and roll, all we do to reset the offense is pass the ball back out on the top to the player in that area. The players on the wings cut, the player on the left screens for the player on the right, and the offense continues the same as before.

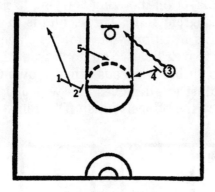

Diagram 1-15

OPTIONS

One of the best things about the Multiflex Offense is you always have two or more options on all cuts. These options should be explained to your players. Through repetition your players will learn to look for these automatically.

Tell your players that their first option is "look to shoot." You want them to have confidence that they can shoot whenever they are open and within their range. You as the coach must let them know what their range is. It's rare to find a player who thinks he can't shoot from 20 feet. You must set your players' limits. They may not like it, but you are the one who has to live with it. The main reason to tell them to look to shoot is to make sure that they square to the basket whenever they have the ball. This move puts pressure on the defense and will actually lead to some easy baskets because your players will be better able to find the open man.

The player's second option is "look to pass." Encourage your players to look for the open man, especially those who are closer to the basket.

Finally, their third option is "look to drive." Players must realize that they should not put the ball on the floor unless it is absolutely necessary. Once the ball is on the floor they should not stop dribbling until they know what they are going to do with it—shoot or pass. There are only two times a player who receives a pass in the front court should dribble the basketball. The first is to improve his passing angle. This will usually occur when a player on the wing is trying to get the ball into the low post (Diagram 1-16). The second is to take the ball to the basket. In this situation, you want the player to always get there in one or two dribbles. You don't want the player using more than two dribbles because this allows the defense to recover and adjust to all moves and will usually result in a charging foul by the offensive man (Diagram 1-17).

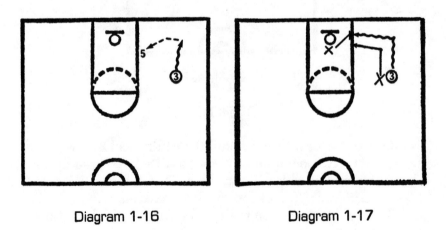

Diagram 1-16   Diagram 1-17

As you initiate the offense, the two options immediately available are the wings breaking out to the side (Diagram

1-18). Because one wing will be screening for the other they will get to the wing area at slightly different times. This gives the point guard an opportunity to look for both. It is important that the point guard does not favor one side over the other, that he goes to both sides approximately the same number of times. Most players tend to go to the right. By encouraging your point guard to keep it balanced he will be more conscious of going to both sides.

When the ball is on the wing the options open to the offense are: the give and go, with the point and wing, and the strongside post on the box (Diagram 1-19).

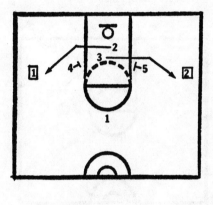

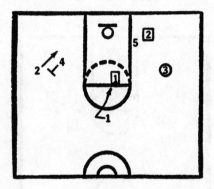

Diagram 1-18   Diagram 1-19

The strongside wing next looks for the weakside wing coming off the screens on the opposite side (Diagram 1-20). The wing then looks for the open man coming off the interchange between the posts (Diagram 1-21).

When the weakside post sets a screen for the strongside wing, there are four options available. The first is the shot by the wing as he comes off the screen (Diagram 1-22). The second is the post rolling to the basket or high-post area (Diagram 1-23). The third option is the weakside post on the "duck-in" move (Diagram 1-24). The fourth is the player [(1) in Diagram 1-25) coming off the screen on the weak side (Diagram 1-25).

Coaching Point: Stress that the wing should wait for the second post to come across the lane before the ball is passed back out on top to start the offense over again. Most players

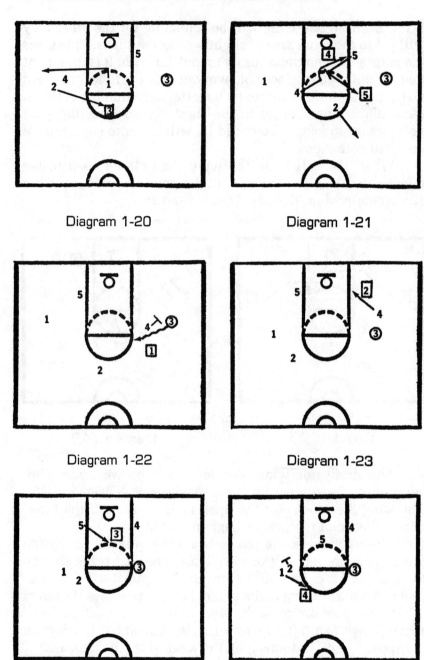

Diagram 1-20

Diagram 1-21

Diagram 1-22

Diagram 1-23

Diagram 1-24

Diagram 1-25

feel that they must rush and will often pass the ball back out on top before the weakside post has had a chance to come to the ball. Good defensive teams will not allow you to get a shot in low right away. With patience on the part of your players, things will open up as they wait for their teammates to make their cuts.

This is the basic set, cuts, and options of the Multiflex Offense. In teaching it, it is best to have the players move through it slowly. The tendency at first will be to rush through it—this will upset the timing. Preach and practice patience and execution. Make sure that the players make all cuts on "balance." Everyone must be under control. Be quick, but don't hurry.

The actual drills used to teach the offense will be covered later in Chapter 13.

Before you take the offense any further you will want to make sure that the players run the offense smoothly and are confident and comfortable in what they are supposed to do. It is necessary to have this strong foundation before you take them to the next level.

You may be surprised how quickly your players will be able to adapt to this offense. High school coaches who have only a brief period of time to put in an offense before beginning their season will find this offense particularly satisfying. The basic sets and cuts can be easily learned by your players in less than two weeks.

2

Optional Multiflex Sets

The Multiflex Offense will work effectively against most of the teams you'll face. The average defender will not be able to stay with his man through the series of screens, allowing your team to start the offense where you wish. Occasionally you will face the team that plays super defense. If you start the offense the same way each time against this team, the opposing players will eventually start to overplay the things you want to do, forcing your team to get the ball further from the basket than you want, or even worse, prevent you from running the offense at all. At such times, you'll need to consider choosing another offensive option.

FIVE BASIC OPTIONS OF THE MULTIFLEX OFFENSE

One of the best things about the Multiflex Offense is that it can be started five different ways without changing the basic rules and cuts. They are: (1) The Basic Cuts and Screens, (2) High Post, (3) Double High Post, (4) Rotate, and (5) Fast Break.

The first option was described in Chapter 1. The wings exchange positions using the posts and each other to free themselves to start the offense. As noted, against most teams this will probably be the only way you ever need to get into the offense. Let's examine the remaining four options more closely.

High Post

The second way to start the offense is called "high." The call can either be made verbally or with a hand signal by the point guard. The call must be made early enough so that the other players will know what to do before they make their cuts. As the point guard [(1) in Diagram 2-1] brings the ball into the attack area, just above the top of the key, (4) starts to move out to the side as if he is going to set the screen for the wing. Instead, (4) now breaks to the high-post position. At the same time the wing on that side takes his man out another step away from the basket, then makes a hard backdoor cut. The opposite wing hesitates, then cuts hard off (5)'s screen (Diagram 2-1). This hesitation will prevent him from taking his man into the backdoor cut and allowing the defender to help out. If neither (4) nor the wing on his side is open on their initial cuts, the two wings exchange as before with the wing on (4)'s side setting the pick for the opposite wing (Diagram 2-2). From here the offense is run just as before. The post, on the side of the pass, posts up low, the opposite post breaks up high (after screening for the wing) and the point and wing exchange (Diagram 2-3).

On the initial cut, if the wing is open (1) should hit him with a pass. The timing on this is crucial and your team will have to spend some time practicing this. The pass should be thrown by (1) to the near side of the basket—this prevents the weakside defenders from helping out. The timing of the pass should be that the ball reaches the wing just as he steps into the lane.

If (4) is open on his cut to the high post, (1) has the option of getting the ball to him there. When the pass is made into the high post the players must now make the following cuts: (1) breaks opposite the ball. The wing on (4)'s side sets a pick for the opposite wing coming across the lane. As (4) catches the ball, he must pivot and face the basket. This will allow him to see who is open off the various cuts. As the wings exchange and neither one is open they should continue to the wing areas (Diagram 2-4).

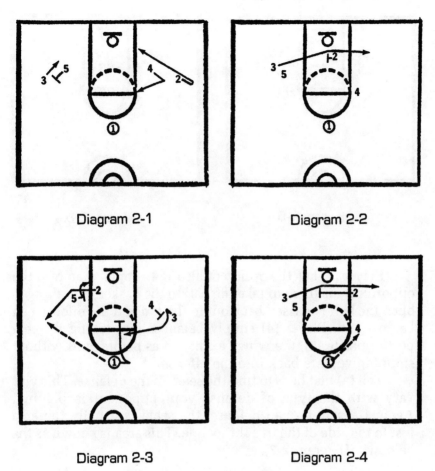

Diagram 2-1

Diagram 2-2

Diagram 2-3

Diagram 2-4

The post on the weak side now sets a pick for the wing coming across the lane. You will find that this is an extremely effective move, screening for the screener. As the wing comes off the pick he should be looking for a possible pass from the high post. At the same time (5) should make a "duck in" move to the ball and then cross the lane so that he is on the same side as (4) but only in the low-post position (Diagram 2-5).

If no one is still open (1) continues to the weak side and headhunts the defender covering the wing on that side. The strongside wing is in the wing area and (5) is on the box (Diagram 2-6).

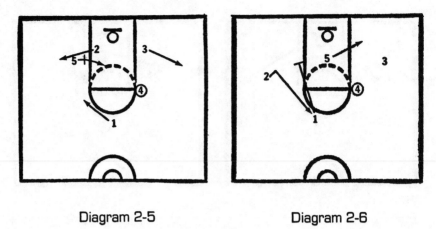

Diagram 2-5   Diagram 2-6

Player (4) has the option of hitting the open man or if the opportunity is there to take the ball to the basket. If nothing is open the ball is passed back out to the top and the offense can begin again. Player (4) simply balances out, taking the low post opposite (5), the wings exchange as before, and without stopping you are back into the offense.

Tell (4) that he is to find the seam in the defense. This will vary with the type of defense your opponent is playing. Against a man-to-man defense, the seam is usually the area just to the side of the free throw line. This area is known as the "elbow" (Diagram 2-7).

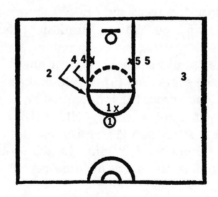

Diagram 2-7

While playing against zones the seam will usually be the middle of the free throw line. Diagrams 2-8, 2-9, and 2-10 show the seams in the 2–1–2, 2–3, and 1–2–2 zones respectively.

The one exception here is the 1–3–1 zone. Against this defense, the seam is again the elbow of the free throw line, just as in the man-to-man defense (Diagram 2-11).

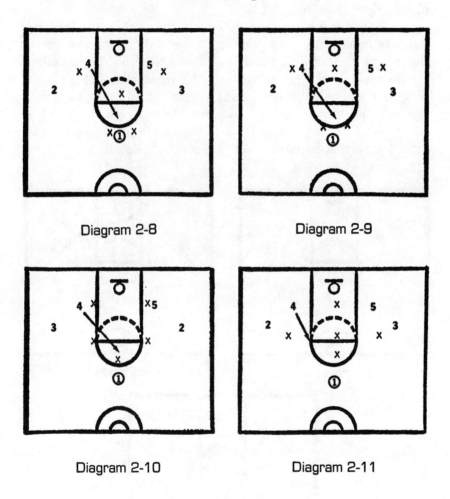

Diagram 2-8   Diagram 2-9

Diagram 2-10   Diagram 2-11

Double High Post

The second variation in starting the offense is called "double." When this is called or signaled, both posts now break up to the high-post area, one on each side of the free throw line. Again they start out to the side as if they are going to set picks for the wings, then they break hard to the elbow (Diagram 2-12).

As in "high," the wings take their men out another step and then cut hard to the basket. If neither wing is open on the backdoor cut, the wing on the left sets the screen for the wing on the right (Diagram 2-13).

Whenever the ball goes to one of the posts the following cuts are made: the wing coming to that side continues out to the wing area, but on a flatter cut than before. While the other wing breaks to the far wing area, the weakside post makes a diagonal cut to the basket, and the point guard cuts away from the ball and moves to set a pick for the wing on the far side (Diagram 2-14). If nothing is open the ball is passed out to the top, the players balance out the floor and the offense simply continues.

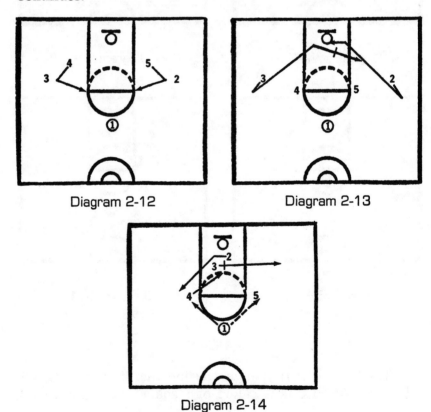

Diagram 2-12   Diagram 2-13

Diagram 2-14

Rotate

The fourth way to start the offense is off the dribble. The point guard calls "rotate," or makes a circular motion with his hand. He then drives the ball to one of the wing spots. The wing on that side cuts backdoor, using the back pick of the post. At the same time the weakside post should set a screen on the topside for the opposite wing, who breaks to the middle of the free throw line (Diagram 2-15).

From here the offense is exactly the same as before. The strongside post cuts to the area up above the box and the weakside wing cuts off the double screen set by the weakside post and the man coming off the point (Diagram 2-16).

If the post doesn't receive a pass from the player on the wing by the count of two, he then clears setting a pick for the weakside wing, who has the option of either cutting high or low across the lane (Diagram 2-17).

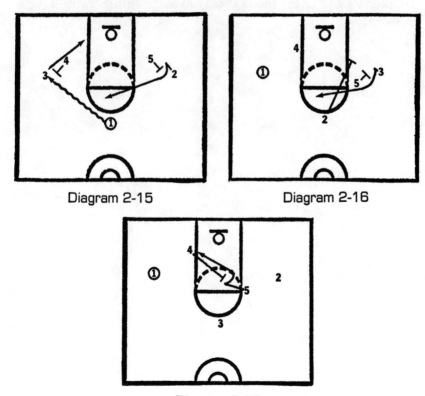

Diagram 2-15   Diagram 2-16

Diagram 2-17

Fast Break

The fifth way to start the offense is off the fast break. This aspect of the offense will be covered in much greater depth in Chapter 10.

Briefly, we have found the designated break to be very complimentary to the Multiflex Offense. This break allows us to have players in specified areas at the end of the break. In turn, with the players already in the same positions at the end of the break as they would be in the start of the offense, we can move smoothly from the break into our offense without having to stop and set up.

Having a variety of optional sets is a necessary part of any offense. Without it your opponent can overplay your initial cuts and force your players further out to start the offense and take you away from everything you are trying to do. It is extremely important that you practice this aspect of the offense. Chapter 13 will cover the best way to teach this to your players in practice.

3

Reading Defenses

One of the keys to the Multiflex Offense is teaching your players how to read the defense. By reading the defense your players will be able to take advantage of any defensive adjustments your opponents may make during the course of a game. This chapter will cover most of the defensive adjustments that your team will probably see as teams try to counter the Multiflex Offense. Like everything else these situations must be practiced until the reads become second nature to your ball club.

POINT GUARD READS

Point Overplay

The first read has to be made by the point guard. Many teams will attempt to force the point guard to one side or the other. When the point feels this pressure he must take his man to the basket, driving down the middle of the lane.

Coaching Point: To set his man up properly the point should fight the pressure by trying to take the ball to the side the pressure is coming from. As the point guard gets the defender to back up he must now react and take the ball to the basket (Diagram 3-1).

As (1) penetrates, the wings must move out to beyond the top of the key for defensive balance. At the same time both posts now roll to the box. By always going to the box, the point guard always knows where a teammate is and can even make a blind pass to the area if necessary. By the time the point has reached the broken circle he should know if he can take the ball all the way to the basket, pull up and take the jumper, or dish the ball off to one of the posts for a lay-up (Diagram 3-2).

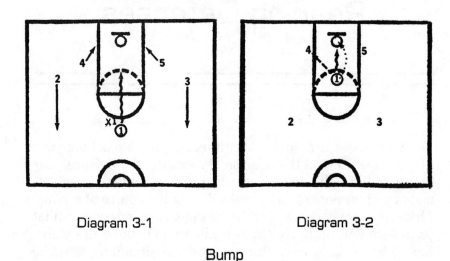

Diagram 3-1   Diagram 3-2

Bump

The second thing we teach our players to read is the play of the defensive wings. If the defenders anticipate the cut across the lane by either of the wings jumping over the screen of the post, we tell the wing to "bump" the post. The wing [(2) in Diagram 3-3] does this by pushing post man (5) in the chest

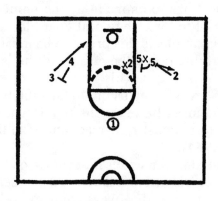

Diagram 3-3

with both hands. This signals the post to turn into the lane and look for the wing's defensive man, preventing him from recovering to the wing, who has stepped back out to the wing area. After screening, the post now pivots to the ball and posts up on the box, looking for a possible pass from the wing. The opposite wing [(3)] must also read this move and break back out to his original side (Diagram 3-3). One of two things will usually happen on the "bump." The wing will either be wide open for a shot or the defenders will be forced to switch creating a mismatch for the post on the box.

Step Over

The next place we tell the wings to read is on the screen set in the lane as the wings exchange. Two things may happen here. First, the defender covering the wing who is setting the screen may hesitate a step on the cross, momentarily backing off of the screen. When the screening wing [(2) in Diagram 3-4] sees this he should "step over" in front of his man and to the ball (Diagram 3-4). This move is executed by having your player take a long step up the lane toward the ball and in turn placing his body between his man and the ball. As he does this he should call for the ball, placing his elbows at shoulder height and his hands up by his face. If (1) passes him the ball, (2) should *immediately* square up to the basket. His options here are the same as the point guard has when he

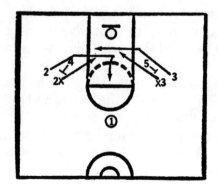

Diagram 3-4

penetrates—drive to the basket, shoot the jumper, or pass the ball to one of the posts who have moved to the box* (Diagram 3-5). If the wing doesn't receive a pass from the point, he must move to the wing area and the offense continues as before.

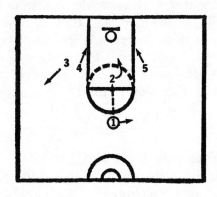

Diagram 3-5

The second thing that can happen as the wings exchange is a defensive switch. Whenever the defenders switch on the exchange, we want the wing [(2)] who set the screen to "freeze." He does this by using a reverse pivot up the lane toward the ball. By pivoting on his foot closest to the ball, the wing will have the defender on his back, and in a position in the lane to receive a pass from the point. If he gets the ball from (1) his options are the same as before: Shoot the jumper, pass to either of the posts, or continue in for a layup (Diagram 3-6).

As the wings continue across the lane they must be aware of their man's position. If the defensive man is trailing behind the wing trying to avoid the post's pick, we want the wing [(2) in Diagram 3-7] to "curl" around the post and up the side of the lane toward the ball (Diagram 3-7). If the pass is made here the wing must again square to the basket and either shoot, pass the ball off to one of the posts, or drive to the basket. If he doesn't receive a pass, the wing breaks out to the side, trying to rub his man off of the post on that side as he does so (Diagram 3-8).

---

*Note: The Player must be conscious of the 3-second rule and make his move immediately upon catching the ball.

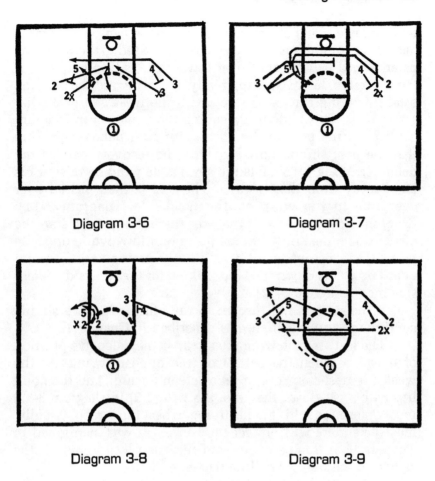

Diagram 3-6

Diagram 3-7

Diagram 3-8

Diagram 3-9

Fade

If the wing's defensive man tries to beat the wing by going over the top of the post's screen, we want the wing [(2) in Diagram 3-9] to "fade." He does this by flattening out his cut and moving to the corner. In order for this to be effective, the point guard must make a hard lob pass to the corner, so that the defense does not have a chance to recover to that area (Diagram 3-9).

Weakside Bump

The next area we want the players to read is the play of the weakside defenders. The point must be made here that with today's man/help defenses, this move can be extremely helpful to your offense. After the ball is passed to the wing, the defense will usually shift over toward the ball to help out. If the weakside defensive wing really cheats toward the ball, the weakside wing runs a "bump" with the weakside post (Diagram 3-10). This is done by having the wing [(2) in Diagram 3-10] push the post in the chest with both hands, signaling that the post should now step into the recovery path of the defender. Wing (2) signals the strongside wing by raising his hand away from the baseline. The ball is then passed over everyone to the wing on the weakside (Diagram 3-11). Everyone now moves as if that was the initial pass to start the offense. The post on that side [(5)] posts low, while opposite post (4) moves out to set a pick for the wing and the point guard now cuts down the lane looking for the weakside defensive man (Diagram 3-12).

If the pass is not thrown to the other wing, we simply continue to run the offense as described in Chapter 1.

The last area the wing must read is the defensive position of his man when the ball is on the opposite wing. As the weakside post steps out to set a screen for him, and the point begins his cut down the lane, the wing [(3) in Diagram 3-13] must determine if his man is trying to beat the screen. Usually, most defenders will protect the basket, as was mentioned in Chapter 1. In this case we want the wing [(2)] to cut off the screen to the free throw line (Diagram 3-13).

Occasionally, the defensive wing will try to go over the top of the screen in an attempt to cut off the pass to wing (2) at the free throw line. When this happens the wing [(2)] automatically cuts hard backdoor to the basket, signaling the strongside wing by raising his hand as he cuts. The point guard must also be aware of this read by now making his cut behind the wing's defender and in turn preventing the defense from recovering to the backdoor cut (Diagram 3-14).

If nothing is open on this read, the wing cuts back out to the top, and the point moves out to the weakside wing position (Diagram 3-15).

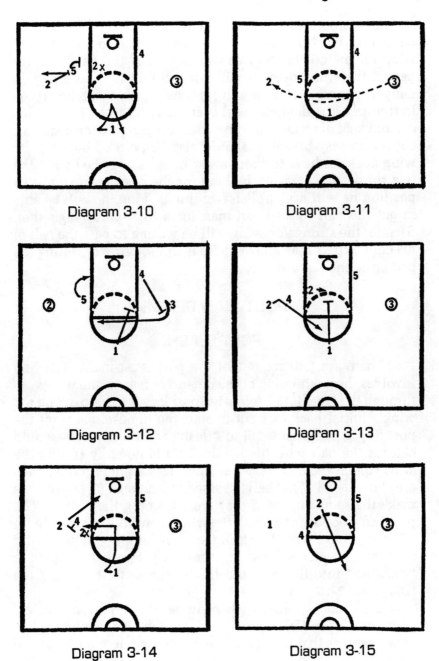

Diagram 3-10

Diagram 3-11

Diagram 3-12

Diagram 3-13

Diagram 3-14

Diagram 3-15

It is important to emphasize here that this read will only happen if the strongside wing passes the ball to the opposite wing on his cut to the free throw line. If the ball is never passed there, the defense will not feel that it is necessary to deny this move. But if the wing is consistently receiving a pass in this area, the defender will eventually try to anticipate this cut and beat his man to the area, thus opening up the backdoor cut for an easy basket. It should also be pointed out that the wing does not have to shoot every time he gets the ball in the free throw line area. By looking for the open man from this position he will accomplish two things. First, he will be able to get the ball to an open man for a high-percentage shot. Second, the strongside wing will be willing to pass the ball to his counterpart if he knows there is a possibility of getting the ball back once in a while.

POST MAN READS

POST FLASH

There are four reads that the post must make. The first involves the positioning of the defensive man as the wings cut through the lane. If the defensive post leaves to help out on the wing's initial backdoor cut to start the offense, we want the post [(5) in Diagram 3-16] to "flash" up the lane. He should call for the ball with his hands. This is done by raising the arms so that the elbows are at shoulder height and the hands are at face level. If the ball is passed to post man (5) the players make the same cuts as if they were running the "high." The point cuts opposite the ball, the wings continue to cross, (with wing (3) coming to the strong side making a slightly flatter cut), and weakside post (4) screening for the wing, then "ducking" into the lane and finally across to the strongside (Diagrams 3-16, 3-17).

If a situation arises where none of the players can get open on their initial cuts we tell (4) that he is the safety valve. When he sees that no one is free he breaks out to a position to get the ball. At times he may have to go beyond the top of the circle to get open. When he gets the ball, he simply gets the ball back to the point guard or one of the wings, and we start over (Diagram 3-18).

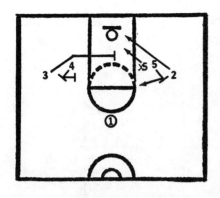

Diagram 3-16

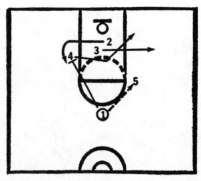

Diagram 3-17

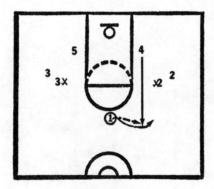

Diagram 3-18

Countering the Defense Post

The next read by the post is the way the defender tries to get into his defensive position when the ball is passed to his side. If the defensive post tries to step over the top of the post, (this is the way most players will defend this situation), we want our post to pivot forward on the foot closest to the free throw line and try to ride the defender up higher with his hip (Diagram 3-19). If the defender tries to get into a deny position by going around the post on the baseline side, our post must now reverse pivot into the defender's path, keeping him on the strongside post's backside (Diagram 3-20).

The last thing a defensive post can do is just play behind

our post. In this case we tell the post to make a reverse pivot and at the same time take a half step up the lane (Diagram 3-21).

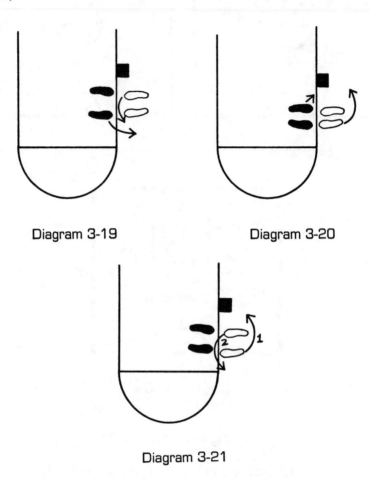

Diagram 3-19   Diagram 3-20

Diagram 3-21

Passing the Ball Inside

The post must always keep his knees bent and his free arm and hand extended calling for the ball. The arm on the side of the defender should be up, parallel to the floor and bent so that the elbow is in the defensive man's chest.

Coaching Point: This is the position we teach every player to hold whenever he is in a post-up situation, whether that player is posting up on the box or at midcourt. Second, we tell the player with the ball to throw the ball to the free hand. If the player posting up does not have his hand up calling for the ball, then *don't* throw it to him. In fact we use this as our signal between the post and the wing who has the ball. When the post drops his hand down, he is now going to move across to set the screen for the other post.

Whenever the defensive post fronts our strongside post, we want the post to step into the defender with his top foot, keeping his arm closest to the defensive man parallel to the floor. The elbow of this arm should be placed in the middle of this man's back, between the shoulder blades. It is important that the post keep his arm bent, preferably to the point where he can grab his own jersey. This will prevent him from pushing off of the defensive man when he goes to get the ball. The wing should throw the ball at the near corner of the backboard, and not at his teammate's hand. As the ball passes over the post's head he should release and go after it, not before (Diagram 3-22).

In passing the ball into the post it is very important that the wing read the position of the defensive post's arm. If the defender's arm, with which he is trying to deny the pass, is below the post's arm, the wing must use a hard lob pass to the strongside post's free hand. If the defender's arm is above the post's, then the wing should throw a quick bounce pass away from the defender. Whenever the wing [(2) in Diagram 3-23] passes the ball inside he must move; he cannot just stand there. We generally want him to move toward the free throw line and set a pick for the offensive player at the top of the key (Diagram 3-23). We tell him that if he sees his man constantly doubling down on the post that he should now move to the corner, where the post can dump the ball back out to him for a short jumper (Diagram 3-24).

Whenever the ball is passed inside we want the other post [(4) in Diagram 3-25] to immediately go to the box on the weakside, while weakside wing (1) must go to the corner of the free throw line (Diagram 3-25). This will keep the offensive players moving without the ball and at the same time the strongside post will always know where his teammates are on

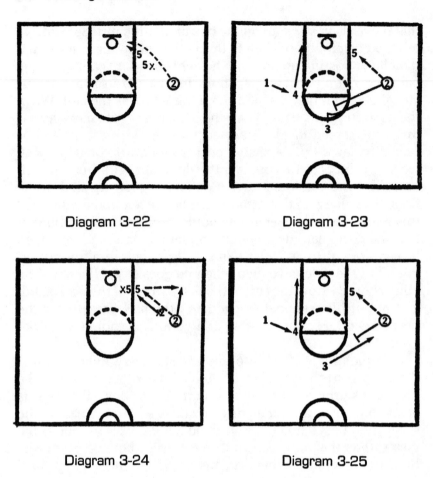

Diagram 3-22   Diagram 3-23

Diagram 3-24   Diagram 3-25

the court. It is important to teach the post that he must pass the ball back out to a teammate whenever he feels strong defensive pressure from more than one player. By passing the ball back out it keeps all the players in the game, and in turn they will be more willing to pass the ball back inside as the game and season go on.

Weakside Post Flash

The last read the posts have to make is the play of the weakside post's defensive man. Whenever this defender sags in to help out on the strongside post, the opposite post [(4) in

Diagram 3-26] must immediately break across the lane to the ball. If he is open on this cut the wing should throw him the ball as soon as he is free. This will get him the ball in scoring position. When this pass is made, the rest of the players make the following cuts: point man (3) and weakside wing man (1) exchange, strongside wing (2) moves to an open area toward the corner, and strongside post (5) reverse pivots pinning his defender on his back (Diagram 3-26). As the point and weakside wing exchange [(3 for 1) in Diagram 3-27] one of them sets a pick for the other. We prefer the down pick to free the player coming off the wing for a jumper, but setting a back pick [(1 for 3)] for the player on the point is equally effective (Diagrams 3-27, 3-28).

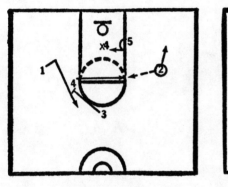

Diagram 3-26

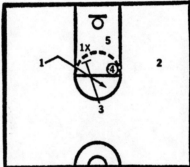

Diagram 3-27

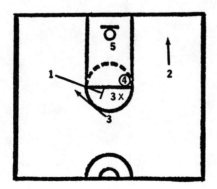

Diagram 3-28

The reads are the same against both man-to-man defense and zones. Both of these will be covered in greater detail later. As with all aspects of basketball these reads must be practiced until they become second nature to the players. Although it may seem like there are many different situations to read they are quite simple to learn because they follow basic basketball logic and instincts. You will find that the players adapt very quickly to the offense and the different defensive moves they are being taught.

It cannot be emphasized enough that making the proper reads is a key to the success of this offense, and that with time and practice your players will be able to rip apart *any* defense.

4

Using the Multiflex against Defensive Overplay

THE BACKDOOR SERIES

The last few years have seen the strong defensive overplay of the forwards, or wings, forcing their counterparts to receive the ball further from the basket. This forces the offense to start out much further away from the basket than the offense would like. The defender, in order to accomplish this, must play another step or more on the top side of the offensive wing. In order to get open, the wing must have some counter moves available to him or be forced to receive the ball way out on top. The Multiflex Offense has a number of backdoor moves to overcome this defensive overplay and thus allow your team to not only start the offense where you would like, but also to get the ball in excellent scoring position against this type of defense. Often the success you have in running the backdoor series will force opponents to change their defense, allowing your team to run the more conventional set and cuts.

Backdoor off the Initial Cuts

The first backdoor series comes off of the initial cuts made by the wings. As the wings cut off the screens set by (4) and (5) they must be aware of the position of the men covering them on defense. If their man gets caught in the screen by the post, the wing continues hard to the basket, looking for a pass

37

from the point guard. They should help the point guard in finding them by calling for the ball with their hand closest to the basket, raising it out in front of them, and giving the point guard a target. The point guard must also be aware of the weakside defenders who may position themselves in the lane (Diagram 4-1). The point guard can help himself here again by keeping his head directly on the basket, allowing him to see both sides of the court equally well.

If nothing is open off of this initial cut, the wings should continue across the lane, looking for the next screen, and into the regular offense. After continuing to the wing area, and a pass is made to start the offense, the rest of the reads and cuts are still the same as they were before. It is very important that the wings run their cuts close to the other wing and the posts so that they are able to get open in an area where we want the ball (Diagram 4-2).

It will be necessary for you and your staff to work this into your regular practice routine. The players must be able to recognize the defensive overplay and their proper response to it automatically.

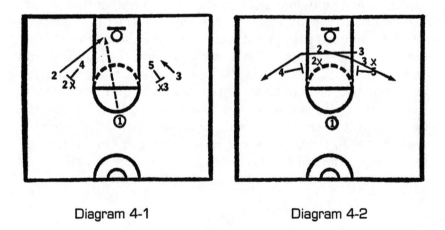

Diagram 4-1   Diagram 4-2

Backdoor from the High Series

The second place we look for a backdoor cut is off the "high" series. In fact, if we feel the players are having a difficult time starting the offense in the designated areas, we will call this set in order to force them to be more aware of the backdoor opportunities. Although this was covered in some detail in Chapter 2, it is important enough to be repeated here. As the point guard brings his man into the top of the key, (4) should break up to the free throw line area. He must start out as if he is going to set a pick for the wing on his side and then suddenly break to the line. Against man-to-man defenses this will be the area at the corner of the free throw line, or the "elbow," while against some zones, 2–3, 2–1–2, and 1–2–2, it will be the center of the free throw line. For now we will assume it is the man-to-man defense. As (4) breaks up to the top, the wing on his side [(2) in Diagram 4-3] should take his man out another step and then cut hard to the basket (Diagram 4-3). As in the last backdoor series, the wing should call for the ball with his baseline hand, and the point guard must keep his head on the center of the basket to pick up any defenders who may be sagging into the lane.

If the wing is open the point guard must get him the ball soon enough so that he can catch and shoot it. If the point guard passes the ball late, the wing will either be caught under the basket or the weakside defenders will be able to recover and pick up the wing with the ball. We prefer that the point guard get the ball to the wing a step and a half to two steps in front of the basket (Diagram 4-4).

It is important that the other wing do two things to help ensure the success of the backdoor cut. The first thing to do is to hesitate a count before making a cut across the lane. This

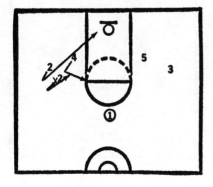

Diagram 4-3

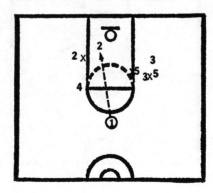

Diagram 4-4

will also give him a chance to see what is happening and make an appropriate move. Second, the wing must flatten out his cut across the lane so that he doesn't take his man into the area of the possible pass. He must still look for the opposite wing defender and set a screen on this man (Diagram 4-5).

If nothing is open off the backdoor cut, the wings should continue out to the wing area and into the regular offense. As before, they must run their men into the screens set by each other and by the posts.

Backdoor from the Double Set

You can also run a backdoor series off the "double" set. The offense starts as before, with the posts stepping out to set screens for the wings. Now, however, the posts both break up to the "elbow" of the free throw line, before the wings make their cuts. As in "high," the wings must take their defenders out another step away from the basket. It is preferable that the wing on the same side as (4) break to the basket first, as in Diagram 4-6. This eliminates the possibility of both players getting to the basket at the same time. As before, the other wing must hesitate a count before he breaks to the basket. He must also make a flatter cut to the basket to prevent his defender from recovering to the ball if a pass is made to the other wing (Diagram 4-6). If you prefer you can use another rule as to which player breaks to the basket first. Some coaches may

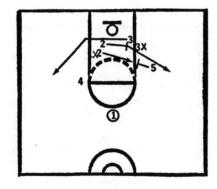

Diagram 4-5

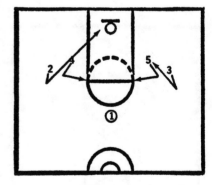

Diagram 4-6

like the idea of having the wing on the right always cut first. The important thing here is to have a rule that all the players understand and feel comfortable with.

Backdoor from the Wing

The next three areas we will run a backdoor series from are after the ball has been passed to the wing. The first person we want to look for the backdoor opening is the point guard. After the point guard passes the ball, he should be alert to the reaction of the man covering him. If that defender either turns his head looking for the ball or doesn't move with the point guard as he makes his cut, the point should cut hard to the basket and call for the ball by raising his hand. The wing should now look to see if he can get him the ball by throwing a hard lob pass to the far side of the basket (Diagram 4-7). Just like the point guard, the wing must be sure to look at the whole picture by keeping his head straight on the basket. This will allow him to see all of the defenders equally well, and should prevent him from throwing any questionable passes.

The next person that has the option of making a backdoor cut after the wing has the ball is the weakside wing. If his man cheats into the lane in an attempt to beat him to the spot at the free throw line, the wing should cut hard to the basket, calling for the ball at the same time. By raising his baseline hand, the wing signals that he is cutting backdoor, and also gives his

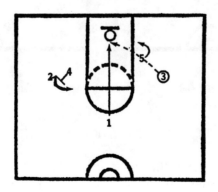

Diagram 4-7

counterpart a target to pass to. Again, if the wing is open, the ball should be passed to the far side of the basket and away from any defenders (Diagram 4-8).

The last person to have an option to cut backdoor from the wing is the weakside post. After both the point guard and weakside wing have made their cuts, the post can now break to the basket if his defender is caught out of position. Whenever the weakside post defender moves more than half-way across the lane and is still above the broken circle, the post should read this and cut to the basket. As the weakside posts cuts he should also call for the ball by raising his hand. If open, the pass should be made to the far side of the basket by the strongside wing (Diagram 4-9). It is very important that the players be taught to throw the ball on a hard lob to the far side of the basket, and slightly in front of the rim. This allows the player who is breaking to the basket to catch the ball and have enough room left to go up with a strong power move and not get caught under the basket after he comes down with the pass.

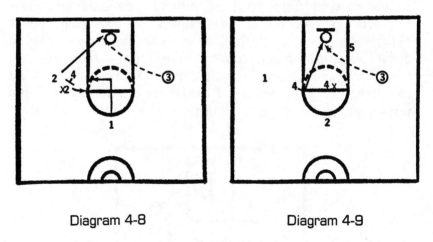

Diagram 4-8   Diagram 4-9

Backdoor from the Flash

The final place that we run a backdoor cut from is off of our "flash" move. Whenever (4) sees that no one can get open, he is to break up to the high-post area. As he breaks up the lane the wing on that side (this will be the wing that has cut to that side off of the initial moves) should set up his defender for his backdoor cut by taking this man away from the basket another step. Once the ball has been passed to (4) in the high-post area, the wing on that side now cuts hard to the basket looking for a pass from (4) (Diagram 4-10). Player (4) should be taught to catch the ball and in turn make a bounce-pass feed to the wing breaking to the basket. A bounce pass will allow the wing to catch the ball easier and will be a much tougher pass for the defender to recover and knock away. After passing the ball inside, the point guard must cut away from the high-post area to prevent his man from doubling down on the post. Our rule is that the wing and the point guard exchange on this sort of a play. At the same time, the weakside post would now "duck in." There will be times, however, against certain opponents, that you may want to run a variation of this play. Whenever your team is getting a lot of strong overplay from the defense, a very effective counter to this is to run a second backdoor cut off of this "flash" move. This is shown in Diagram 4-10. In this case, with the defense set up to stop the weakside screen, we will send the weakside wing backdoor off a screen by the weakside post, and then off of a screen by the strongside wing, who had made the initial backdoor cut. Again, the point guard has cut away from the high post to prevent any double teaming of the ball. After the wing cuts past him, the post on the weakside should again "duck in" looking for the ball. We can easily call this play from the bench by calling out "special" or using some other key to signal the play.

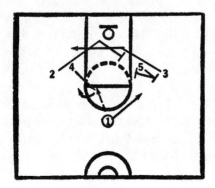

Diagram 4-10

We believe the backdoor series is essential to counter to-day's pressure defenses. We will often use it as a secondary offense against opponents who don't pressure the ball much. The real beauty of it is that it fits naturally into the regular set and cuts of the Multiflex Offense. The main things to remember are: (1) the wings must always take their men out a step or so further from the basket before they make their backdoor cut; (2) as the players cut backdoor they should call for the ball by raising their baseline hand—this alerts the player with the ball that his teammate is going to cut to the basket and at the same time it gives him a target to pass to; (3) the wing on (4)'s side always cuts first and the player opposite him should hesitate one count before cutting across the lane; (4) the player with the ball should keep his head on the basket so that he can see everything develop, including any defensive adjustments— this will also help in preventing him from telegraphing the fact that he is looking at making the backdoor pass; and (5) if nothing is open the players should not force anything, but continue through the regular cuts and screens—eventually something will open up.

It is also important to stress to the players that the backdoor cuts can be made (and should be) anytime the defense tries to overplay an offensive man's regular cut. This may happen off the first, or initial moves, of the offense, or it may come after the team has gone through the offense a couple of times. The key is to recognize the overplay and to counter it immediately. This can only happen through practice and repetition. The timing of the backdoor series is crucial. As the coach, you must learn to live with the rash of turnovers you will see when you first begin practicing this series. But in time, you will see the timing become more precise and its effectiveness against the better defensive teams will become more evident.

Here's one final thought on the backdoor series. You may want to consider using it at the start of the game when your opponent is really pumped up, trying to prevent you from starting the offense. Run properly, it can have a demoralizing effect on the opposition, and in turn, set the tempo for the entire game.

5

The Multiflex Calls

ADVANTAGES OF USING CALLS

We have found that all teams will at one time or another go through a dry spell on offense, or need to take advantage of certain offensive situations that may arise during the course of a game. If you have used a passing game in the past you will know that unless you have another offense to use in these situations, you are virtually helpless to do anything about them.

The Multiflex Offense has a series of calls within the offense that allow you to do what you want yet remain within the structure of your regular offense. The two main advantages this gives you is that it is extremely rare to go for any noticeable time without scoring, and we can take advantage of any opportunity that may present itself during the course of the game.

The calls are made by the point guard after he gets them from the coach. At some point in time you may have a point guard who you trust to call the plays on his own, but in the beginning it is best that you call them for him.

The terms we use are very descriptive, which makes them easy to remember. Later, in another chapter, we will discuss an alternate system for calling plays, but in the beginning it will be much easier to refer to the calls by name. Also, all diagrams will show the calls against man-to-man defense. In Chapter 8, we will show you how these same calls work against zone defenses.

The Calls

Point. When we call "point," we want the point guard to penetrate the lane, taking the ball to the basket. As the point beats his man, the wings break out to a defensive position. They *do not* exchange, they break directly out to the top. The posts immediately break to the box on their side. The point now has the option of taking the ball all the way to the basket, pull up and hit the jumper, or pass the ball to one of the posts for a layup (Diagram 5-1). If nothing is open, (1) simply pulls the ball back out, the wings exchange using the posts as screens, and we're back into our regular offense. The two times you may want to use this is when the point guard is getting a lot of pressure from his defensive man (this will help relieve some of that pressure), and when your point guard is far superior to the defender and you need to score.

Wing. Whenever you have superior talent at one of your wing spots, you may want to take advantage of this by occasionally calling "wing." This signals everyone that we want to get the ball to the wing and clear a side for him. As the ball is passed to the wing [(3) in Diagram 5-2] the post on that side clears to the weakside. At the same time the point guard cuts as before head hunting for the defensive weakside wing. The opposite wing uses this triple screen and breaks out to the free throw line looking for a pass from the strongside wing. If the wing cannot beat his man in two dribbles or less we tell him to

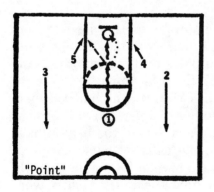

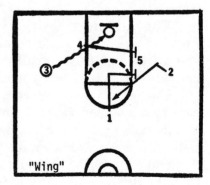

Diagram 5-1   Diagram 5-2

give the ball up, by either hitting the weakside wing coming off the screen, or the point guard who has now moved behind the double screen set by the posts. Diagram 5-2 shows what the "wing" call looks like when the wing beats his man, while Diagram 5-3 shows what it looks like if he can't. If the ball is passed back out and nothing is open the posts balance out the court, the players on the wing exchange and we're back into our offense.

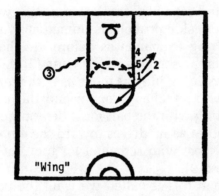

Diagram 5-3

This play is also ideal against the teams that really sag in to help out on defense. By using the double screen on the weakside you will be able to free the point guard for a wide-open shot. One note, if you have an excellent outside shooter, you can use this play to free him behind the screen. The only difference now is that the point guard would start down as if to set a pick, then step back out to the point, and the wing would step behind the screen of the two posts.

Number. If we feel there is a particular defensive player that we can take advantage of we will call a number. The number can either be the position of the player, such as "two," or "five," or it can be the jersey number of a particular player. In either case that player must now post up on the strongside box (using the same post-up position mentioned in Chapter 1), with the post clearing as soon as the ball is passed to his side. The player who posts up must use the same two-count method as the post players. We also use the rule that he has to call for the ball with his free hand, and that once he lowers it, he is no longer in a position to get a pass from the wing. Diagram 5-4 shows the point in the post-up position, Diagrams 5-5 and 5-6 the wings, and Diagrams 5-7 and 5-8 the weakside and strongside posts respectively. All other cuts and moves off of this call should be the same as if we were running the regular offense. When the posting player releases to the weak side he should try to set a pick for the post at the weakside high post.

Continuation. This call signals the weakside post to cut across the lane and set a pick for the strongside wing, who has the ball. The strongside post clears immediately and the point and weakside wing exchange as before. As the post [(5) in Diagram 5-9] sets the screen and the wing (2) puts the ball on the floor, the remaining players move as in the regular offense, the point and wing exchange again and the weakside post ducks in. The wing with the ball must determine who is open within two dribbles as he drives toward the elbow of the free throw line. The post who screened for him now rolls to the basket (Diagram 5-9).

Corner. When this is called we want the point guard to pass the ball to one of the wings then start to break as he has before. This time, however, he should continue through the lane and then to the near corner. He should always try to come as close to the strongside post as possible when he cuts around the post (Diagram 5-10).

Screen. The point guard has to take his man a step or two in one direction as he brings the ball into the attack area. He must now reverse and bring his man back to the other side and into a pick set by the wing on that side. As this is happening the strongside post clears to the weakside, the weakside post ducks into the lane, and the weakside wing breaks out to the top of the key. As the point drives past the wing [(3) in Diagram 5-11] setting the screen, that wing should roll to the near box. As earlier, we want the point to determine what is open by his second dribble after he moves past the screen. His options are to shoot, hit the wing rolling to the box, pass to the weakside post on the "duck in," or to the wing coming out to the top of the key. It is also possible that the strongside post may be open for a lob to the far side of the basket (Diagram 5-11).

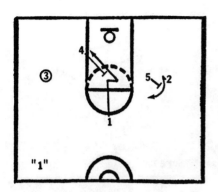

Diagram 5-4

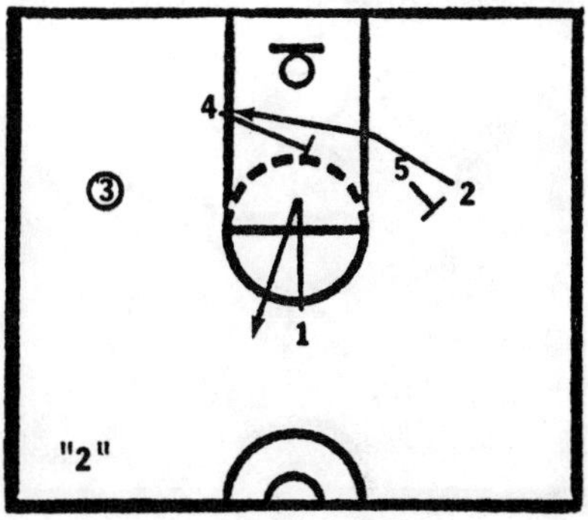

Diagram 5-5

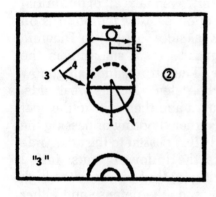
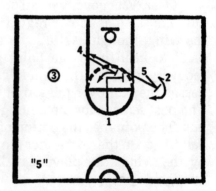

Diagram 5-6

Diagram 5-7

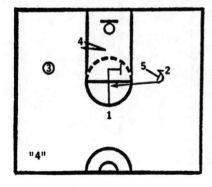
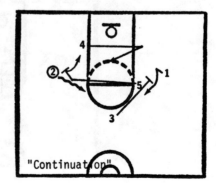

Diagram 5-8

Diagram 5-9

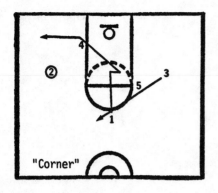

"Corner"

Diagram 5-10

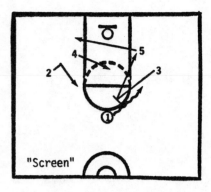

"Screen"

Diagram 5-11

Over. Whenever we call "over," we make all of our initial cuts the same as in our regular offense. After the point is on the wing, though, we tell the weakside post [(5) in Diagram 5-12] to head hunt the point guard's man, standing in the recovery path of the defender. The strongside wing now passes the ball over the top of the defense, to the weak side. The post screens for the point guard and then rolls to the near box. The point has the option of either shooting or passing the ball inside to the post. After the ball is passed to the other side by the wing, the players make the following cuts: initial strongside post (4) screens for wing (2) then moves to the high post opposite the ball, the wing reads the defense and either cuts backdoor or to the free throw line extended, and the wing

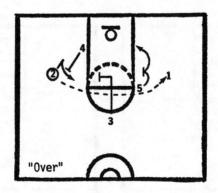

"Over"

Diagram 5-12

at the top of the key cuts down the lane and into the path of the defensive wing (Diagram 5-12).

Low. When the point guard signals "low" it means that we want the wing on the weakside to come across the lane around everyone to the corner on the strong side. This has been preceded by everyone else making the same cuts as they had before. As in "corner," we want the wing [(3) in Diagram 5-13] who is cutting to the weakside to come as close to the post as possible when he makes his cut. This will prevent his man from recovering in time, leaving the wing open as he comes off the screen (Diagram 5-13). The only thing that is run differently here is that the point guard starts to cut down the lane, but then breaks back out to the top after he head hunts the weakside defensive wing.

Step. If you have a post player with good shooting range, "step" may be an excellent play for you. When the ball is passed to the wing, the post [(4) in Diagram 5-14] on that side now steps out away from the lane about three steps. At the same time the weakside post starts to break up to the high post on the weak side then cuts across the lane and down to the box on the strong side. The point and wing exchange as before. The options are the post on the step-out move, or the post moving to the box. The option that will open up the most, though, especially against zones, is the pass to the post in the corner and in turn that post hitting the post on the box (Diagram 5-14).

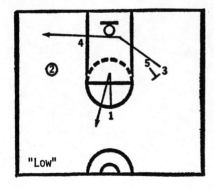

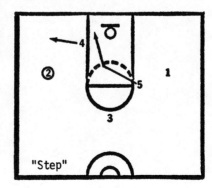

Diagram 5-13   Diagram 5-14

These plays can be very effective against both man-to-man defenses or zones. Chapters 7 and 8 will explain in greater detail what they look like against both man-to-man and zone defenses. It is important that you know when and when not to use these. The offense run properly will usually be all your team needs against most opponents. The calls should be used only when you either find something specific that you want to take advantage of or as a way to prevent a scoring drought. A word of caution: Using the plays too much will probably take away from the continuity of the offense. The players must also realize that the calls are suggestions as to what *might* be open. Do not force passes or shots just because a certain play was called. Your players must learn to take what is open.

6

An Alternate
Numbering System
for the Multiflex

Something that we have gone to the last few years that has proven to be quite successful is a numbering system for our plays instead of verbal calls. There are numerous advantages to using this system. There is more flexibility, the system lends itself well to hand signals, and it is more difficult for the defense to know what you are going to do no matter how many times you call the same play.

NUMBERING THE COURT

We start by numbering areas of the court. The top of the key is 1, the wing area is 2, the corner is 3, (0 if we lob to the far corner), the box is 4, and the lane is 5 (Diagram 6-1).

As we previously explained, the different positions are already numbered, the point guard being (1), the wings (2) and (3), and the posts (4) and (5). By numbering both the players and the court we can now get the ball to any player at any particular spot that we want. The *first* number we call is *always* the player we want to get the ball, while the *last* number we call is *always* the spot where we want him to get the ball.

All of the plays that we discussed in the previous chapter can be run by calling out a number. You are now able to get the ball to the player you want and not just a position. For example, if you wanted to run "point," all you have to do is call "11." This signifies that the point guard [player (1)], is to get the ball at the top of the key and try to beat his man one-on-one (Diagram 6-2). As before, the wings know that they must come out immediately to a position above the top of the circle for defensive purposes.

Now we can take this play one step further. Instead of being limited to just the point guard being able to run "point," we can now call any player's number and we can run "point" with either the wings or the posts. Let's say that our (4) man is quite a bit quicker than the man covering him. In this case we now call "41." This tells the post to break out to the top of the key where he gets the ball from (1). Player (3) would fill in for (4), and (1) and (2) would come back out for defensive balance (Diagram 6-3). Player (4) now must try to take the ball to the basket, keeping the ball in the lane. His options are the same as in "point," drive all the way for the layup, pass off to the players on the box, or stop at the broken circle and take the jumper (Diagram 6-4).

THE CALLS AS NUMBERED PLAYS

The next few pages will show what some of the "regular" calls would look like converted to the numbering system. We will also show you a few of the variations this numbering system opens up for your team. There are many different options you may want to experiment with depending on your personnel.

If we want to run "wing" we would normally call out either "22" or "32," depending on which wing we are trying to free. As before, when the wing receives the ball, the post on that side clears, and along with the point guard and the weakside post sets a triple screen for the weakside wing. After the wing breaks out to the top, the point now steps behind the double screen left by the two posts, and looks for a possible lob pass from the strongside wing (Diagram 6-5).

Now if we have a post man who is a very good one-on-one player, and we are having trouble getting the ball inside to

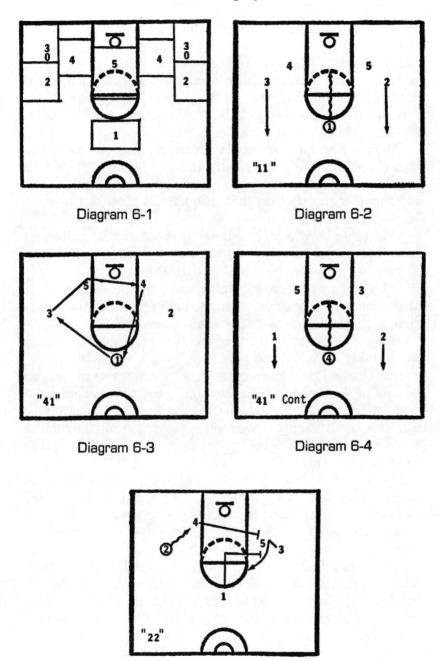

Diagram 6-1

Diagram 6-2

Diagram 6-3

Diagram 6-4

Diagram 6-5

him we may call "52." This tells the post to break out to the wing area for a pass from the point. He does this as the wings exchange sides. The wing opposite (5) does not come across the lane; instead, he hesitates then sets a screen on the lane with the other post. The rest of the play is the same as before, with the wing breaking off the triple screen and the point stepping behind it (Diagram 6-6).

We can also run this play with the point from one of two ways. The first is to simply call "12" and "rotate." This tells everyone that the point guard is going to drive the ball to one side and that the post on that side should clear to the weak side (Diagram 6-7).

The other way to get into the play is to have the point pass the ball to one of the wings and run the offense through until the point is on the wing with the ball (Diagram 6-8).

The first way is much quicker and probably easier, while the second way may actually lead to better continuity with the offense, and subsequently, to easier baskets.

If we want to post up one of the players, instead of calling his "number," we now call his position number with a 4 behind it. This tells that player that he is to post up on the box on the side of the first pass. The one thing the point guard must be aware of is not to pass the ball to the wing we want to post up. If this should happen, we tell the players to run the offense through until we get to the spot where we can get the ball to the wing we want.

Diagram 6-9 shows what the offense would look like if we called a play like "24." Diagrams 6-10 and 6-11 depict the offense if the point guard should happen to pass the ball to the wing we intended to post up. In this case the play would have been "34."

Coaching Point. On all plays that end with an even number, the post on the side of the initial pass must clear to the weak side to open up that particular side. In other words, any play that ends in either "2" or "4," the strongside post (unless he is the player posting up), must always clear the side to open things up. On all other plays, "1," "3," "5," and "0," there should always be a post on the box on the strongside.

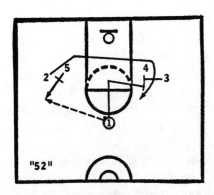

Diagram 6-6

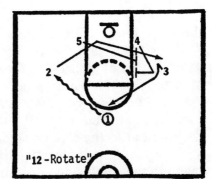

Diagram 6-7

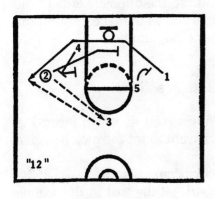

Diagram 6-8

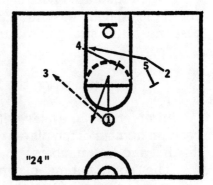

Diagram 6-9

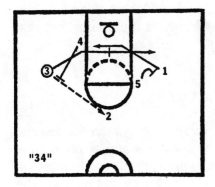

Diagram 6-10

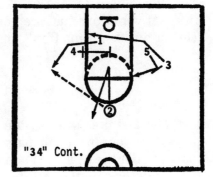

Diagram 6-11

The plays "corner," "low," and "step" are now virtually the same play. "Corner" now becomes "13," "low" is either "23" or "33," and "step" becomes either "43" or "53." In "13," the point guard cuts through the lane and to the corner after passing the ball to one of the wings (Diagram 6-12).

In "23," the wing breaks across the lane, cutting behind everyone to the corner on the strongside, with the point guard backing out to the top for defense (Diagram 6-13).

Play "43" will have two different looks. When the pass is made to the same side as (4), he steps out to the corner to get the ball, and (5) comes across the lane and posts up on the box (Diagram 6-14).

When the initial pass is made to the opposite side of the court, the (4) man must now come across the lane, around the baseline, to the strongside corner (Diagram 6-15).

Numbering the Screen and Roll

In order to run a play with a screen in it, we insert the position number of the player we want to set the pick between the first and last numbers.

The "continuation" play now becomes a play like "252." This means that our (2) player will get the ball in the 2 area, and then receive a screen from (5). Because the play ends with the number 2, the post on that side now clears (Diagram 6-16).

Diagrams 6-17, 6-18, 6-19, and 6-20 show some of the different variations that are possible with the numbering system for our "continuation" play.

Numbering the Lob Plays

The last area we use the numbering system for are the plays that require a lob pass to someone across court or a player under the basket. When we call a lob play with a zero at the end of the call, the call signals the players that we want the ball lobbed to the person, designated by the first number in the

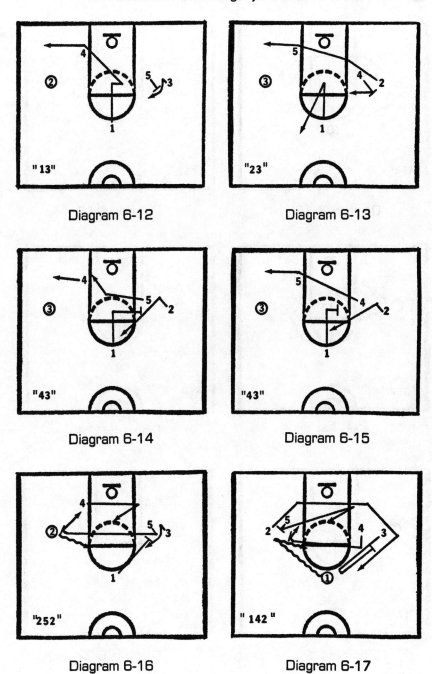

Diagram 6-12

Diagram 6-13

Diagram 6-14

Diagram 6-15

Diagram 6-16

Diagram 6-17

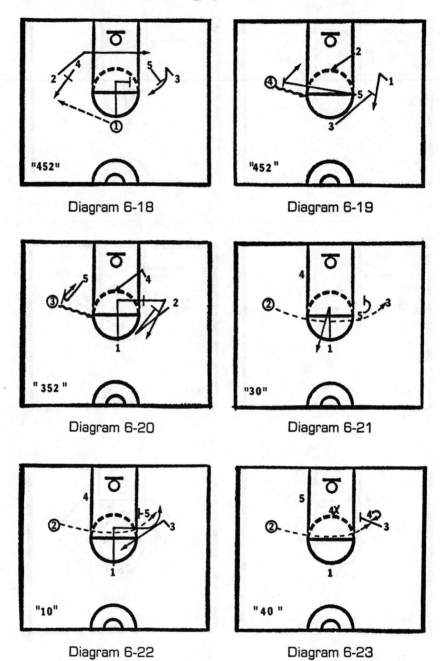

"452"

Diagram 6-18

"452"

Diagram 6-19

" 352 "

Diagram 6-20

"30"

Diagram 6-21

"10"

Diagram 6-22

" 40 "

Diagram 6-23

far corner of the court. For example, when we want to run "over" to our number (3) wing we call out "30." This tells (3) that he is to get a lob pass, in the far corner, from the other wing (Diagram 6-21). As before, the weakside post must set a screen in the recovery path of the man responsible for covering (3). The ball is thrown on a hard lob, so the defender does not have a chance to get back in time to stop (3) from shooting.

Again the numbering system gives us the added flexibility of running this same play with virtually every player on the court. We can run a play for the point guard in the corner, "10" (Diagram 6-22), or for a post, "40" (Diagram 6-23). On the other hand, if we want the ball to go into somebody in the lane, we now call something like "15," "25," or "55" (Diagrams 6-24, 6-25, and 6-26).

It is important that the player throwing the pass into the lane look to see where the weakside defender is playing, and that he throw the pass so that the player receiving it can catch it in front of the basket, for either a layup or a stuff. If the passer throws the ball on a hard lob about one foot in front of the rim, it will enable his teammate to catch the ball and shoot it properly, without having to rush his shot.

You will find this numbering system much more efficient for getting the ball to the player you want and in a location that he can now take advantage of his defensive man.

The calls may be somewhat confusing at first, but you will find the players adjusting to the calls rather quickly after a little practice. One key that will help you to teach the areas is to place the numbers on the floor with tape.

It is important that you stress, (1) the player to receive the ball is *always* the *first* number; (2) that the area where the player is to receive the ball is *always* the *last* number; and (3) if there is a middle number in the call, that is the player who is to set the screen.

This numbering system will add more flexibility to your offense, allowing you greater control in taking advantage of special situations that arise during the course of a game or even a season.

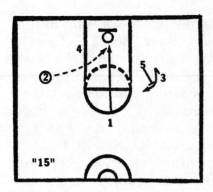

"15"

Diagram 6-24

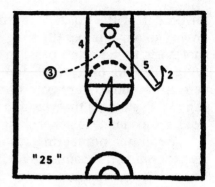

"25"

Diagram 6-25

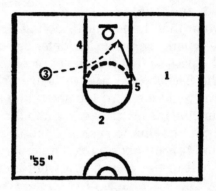

"55"

Diagram 6-26

7

Using the Multiflex against Man-to-Man Defenses

The Multiflex Offense can be used with equal effectiveness against any type of defense. Chapters 7, 8, and 9 will show how the offense should look against man-to-man, zone, and combination defenses respectively. This chapter in particular will serve mostly as a review of the first few chapters; it is important that you understand how the Multiflex should look against each defense so that you, as the coach, can take best advantage of any defensive adjustments that are made.

Diagram 7-1 shows the basic starting position of the players and their initial cuts. The wings must be exchanging by the time the point guard drives his man into the top of the free throw circle. As the wings begin to cut, the posts on their side set a backpick for them. The wing on the left always sets a screen for the wing on the right.

The posts now turn and set screens for the wings coming out of the lane, freeing them for a pass from the point. It is important that the point pass the ball before the wings reach the wing area (Diagram 7-2).

As the wing [(3) in Diagram 7-3] receives the ball he should pivot forward on his inside foot and look to post man (4) who positions himself above the box. The point guard cuts down the lane and into the path of the weakside wing's defensive man. Weakside post (5) sets a back screen for the wing on

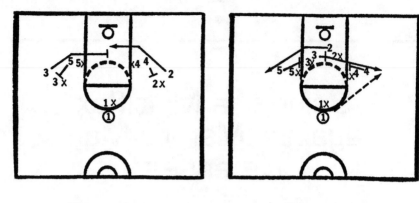

Diagram 7-1   Diagram 7-2

Diagram 7-3

his side and then rolls to the elbow after the wing cuts past him. The weakside wing cuts either to the basket or to the free throw line (Diagram 7-3).

If the strongside post isn't open, he clears to the weak side after "two" counts. He should look for the weakside post's defensive man and screen him. The weakside post has the option of either cutting to the low-post area (Diagram 7-4), or staying high and cutting out to the wing area to set a pick for the wing with the ball (Diagram 7-5). If he screens for the wing, the following cuts are made *as* the wing puts the ball down and drives off the screen. The opposite post "ducks" into the lane, the weakside wing, now on the point, and the

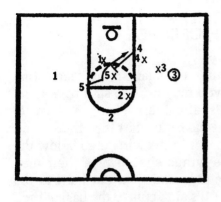

Diagram 7-4

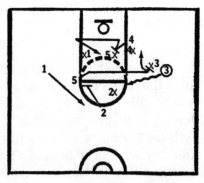

Diagram 7-5

point guard, now on the wing, exchange again. The post setting the screen rolls to the basket.

If the defensive man covering the wing with the ball
overplays the drive to the middle, the wing should make a
power move to the basket. The post in turn rolls to the corner
of the free throw line, the wing and point exchange as before,
and the weakside post again "ducks" into the lane (Diagram
7-6). If no one is open the ball is passed back out to the top and
we start over with the wings (possibly a wing and the point
guard) exchanging as before (Diagram 7-7).

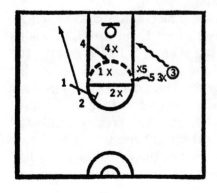

Diagram 7-6

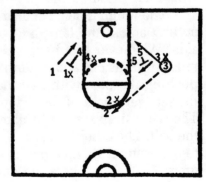

Diagram 7-7

THE MULTIFLEX VS.
THE TOUGH DEFENSE

Whenever your team comes up against the teams that play the really tough defense, you may want to start by emphasizing the backdoor series. Usually these teams will try to force you further away from the basket to start the offense, and will try to deny any entry passes into the wing area below the free throw line extended. The wings should take their men another step or two out to the side and then cut hard to the basket. It is best if the wing on (4)'s side cuts to the basket first, to prevent both players from getting there at the same time. The posts step out and set back screens to help free the wings, and if someone is open, the point should pass the ball to him soon enough so that the weakside defensive men cannot help out (Diagram 7-8).

As the posts set the screen they must be aware of their men helping out on the backdoor cuts. If the defensive post leaves to help out, the post now steps out to the high-post area calling for the ball. When the ball is passed to the high post, he should catch it and pivot toward the basket. As the wings exchange, the player coming to the ball-side must flatten out his cut and move to the near corner. The point guard at the same time cuts opposite the post with the ball, and the weakside post cuts to the broken circle and then to the box on the same side of the ball—the weakside post should cut after the wings have cleared the lane (Diagram 7-9).

The tough defensive teams will also anticipate the wings cutting across the lane, and try to beat them to the opposite side. Whenever this happens the wing [(2) in Diagram 7-10] must stop his cut and "bump" the near post. He does this by pushing the post with both hands. The post now pivots into the recovery path of the defensive wing, and then to the box. The wing simply steps back out to the wing area and calls for the ball. The other wing breaks off his cut and moves back out to his original side, using the screen of the nearside post (Diagram 7-10). From here the offense is exactly the same as before.

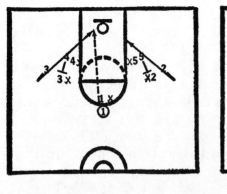

Diagram 7-8

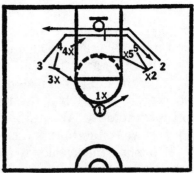

Diagram 7-9

Diagram 7-10

The tough defensive teams will also use a lot of weakside defensive help in trying to prevent the ball from going into the post. They will generally sag someone in on the backside of the strongside post. When this happens the weakside post must cut immediately to the high-post area on the side of the ball, calling for the ball as he cuts across the lane. (When we say calling for the ball, we mean holding his hands up, not a verbal call.) If the ball is passed inside to the post he should pivot and look to the low post who, in turn, should reverse pivot, pinning his man on his back, and then call for the ball with his baseline hand. The strongside wing moves to the near corner, the point and weakside wing exchange, and the strongside post cuts to the weakside box if he isn't open on the pin move (Diagrams 7-11 and 7-12).

The other area that will usually be open against the teams that play the tough defense is on the weak side. The defensive players sag so much that anyone on the opposite side of the ball is wide open. When the players see this, we tell them to run the weakside bump. The weakside wing [(2) in Diagram 7-13] pushes the weakside post with both hands, and then steps back to his wing area. Post (4) then steps into the recovery path of the wing's defensive man. Strongside wing (3) now throws a hard lob pass over the defense to the weakside wing, who then has the option to shoot, hit the post that screened for

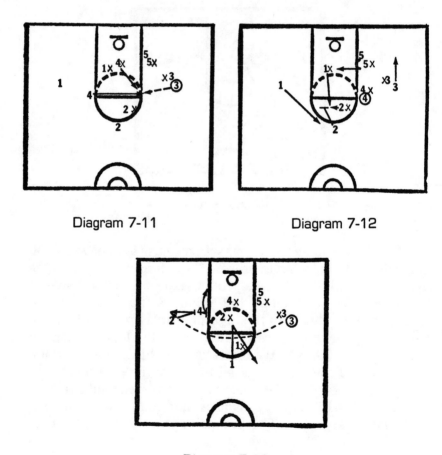

Diagram 7-11   Diagram 7-12

Diagram 7-13

him as he rolls to the box, or hold the ball and run the offense from there (Diagram 7-13).

It is important that your team read the defense and take what is given them; don't force things. By running the offense and looking for the overplays against the tough defensive teams, they will take themselves into an area that they are not able to recover from, leaving someone open for either a backdoor move or an uncontested shot on the side opposite the initial pass.

THE MULTIFLEX VS.
"SOFT" MAN-TO-MAN DEFENSE

There will be teams that play you man-to-man but will allow you to run the offense away from the basket, challenging only inside passes or drives. These teams force you to beat them from the outside. With the Multiflex Offense, the players only have to read the defensive players to get shots from well within their range.

The first area that will usually be open against this type of defense is on the wings. Because the defense is not intent on denying any passes that start the offense, the defensive men will sit back and allow your team to pass the ball to a wing. When this occurs the wings should use the "bump" maneuver and step back out to the wing area. The post pivots into the recovery path of the defensive wing and then rolls to the box. The wing has the option of hitting the post player, shooting, or running the offense from there (Diagram 7-14). It is important that the point guard make his cut down the lane and into the path of the weakside wing's man after he passes the ball to the wing. The defensive man will now be in a poor position to stop his man from getting the ball at the free throw line for the short jumper.

The next place we tell the players to look is on the screen and roll off of the pick by the weakside post. As the wing comes off the screen, the defense will probably get caught behind it leaving the wing with the short jumper from the free throw line (Diagram 7-15). If the defense rotates to help out, the player who will be open is weakside wing point guard (1) coming off the screen set for him by the point, wing (3), or weakside post (5) on the "duck-in" move (Diagram 7-16).

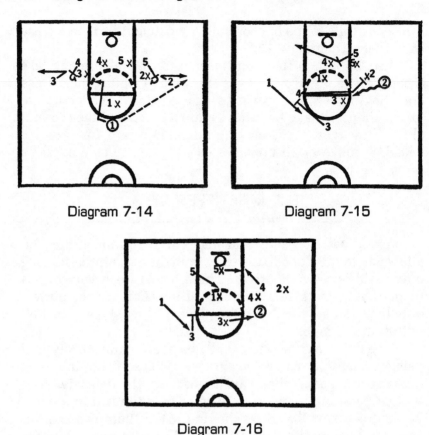

Diagram 7-14

Diagram 7-15

Diagram 7-16

As before, the weakside wing will also be open on the "weakside bump." In fact, with today's defenses, the weakside bump will be open on a regular basis, and your players should be encouraged to look for it. It is very important, however, that the weakside post get himself into a position that blocks the recovery path to the weakside or the better defensive players will be able to recover and, in some cases, even be able to steal the pass.

The Multiflex Offense will get your team excellent shots against any type of man-to-man defense. This is true of many offenses though. With proper execution, most man-to-man offenses will work most of the time. The advantage you will have by running the Multiflex is that you will get excellent shots all the time, and against any man-to-man defense, without having to change offenses.

8

Using the Multiflex against Zone Defenses

One of the best advantages of the Multiflex Offense is that it can be used equally well against any defense, including all types of zone defenses. The main thing that your players must do when playing against a zone is to read the defense. The reads are identical to those made against a man-to-man defense with the following exception: The players must read the defensive man in the area they will be cutting to instead of the defender who is in their present area. By using this simple rule, all the plays and counters become extremely effective against every zone possible.

The following pages will break down the offense against the 2–3 (2–1–2), the 1–3–1, the 3–2, the 1–2–2, and the match-up zones. We will not only cover the basic cuts and the possible openings, but also the most common counters that your team will probably see against each of the above-mentioned defenses.

THE BASIC CUTS AND READS VS. A 2–3 ZONE

The offense begins virtually the same way as it does against the man-to-man defense. The point guard penetrates, drawing the defensive men toward him. The wings begin to exchange, but as they would in "bump," push the post with both hands and pop back out to their original side. The posts should step into the recovery path of the defenders on the top of the key. The point passes the ball to one of the wings [(3) in Diagram 8-1], who then squares to the basket. The post on that side [(5)] rolls to the box, while the opposite post steps up to the high-post area, away from the ball (Diagram 8-1).

The point guard again cuts down the lane looking for a return pass from the wing. The one thing the point guard does differently is that instead of cutting hard through the lane, he should actually walk. By walking right at the defensive man who is now in the middle, this player will usually back up. As the point guard walks directly toward the middle defender, weakside wing (2) hesitates, then cuts to the free throw circle as before (Diagram 8-2). It may be evident that the weakside post did not set a back screen for the wing on his side; it is not necessary for him to do this because there is already a defender in the area of the backdoor move. If post man (4) on the ball-side doesn't receive a pass within two counts he must clear as before. As he clears he looks for the middle man in the zone and screens him. As the weakside wing [(2) in Diagram 8-3] comes across the lane he must be aware of which defender is covering your wing. If the defensive player from the free throw area is covering the ball, the post [(5) in Diagram 8-3] should come across the lane high to the ball (Diagram 8-3). As he comes across the lane, the post should have his hands up, calling for the ball. If he doesn't get a pass from the wing, he should continue out to the side and set a screen on the ball. As before, when the wing puts the ball on the floor, the point and weakside wing exchange (the wing must be sure to step into the recovery path of the defensive guard in the middle of the zone). The original strongside post who has cleared to the weak side "ducks" into the broken circle, and the post who set the screen rolls to the box (Diagram 8-4). As the post rolls he should try to get the inside position on the strongside baseline defender. If nothing is open, the ball is passed back out to the top and we start over.

On the other hand, if the weakside post [(5) in Diagram 8-5] sees that the baseline defender is out covering the wing, he must come across the lane to the box. Most of the time we simply want him to post up (Diagram 8-5), but he has the option to occasionally come all the way across the lane low

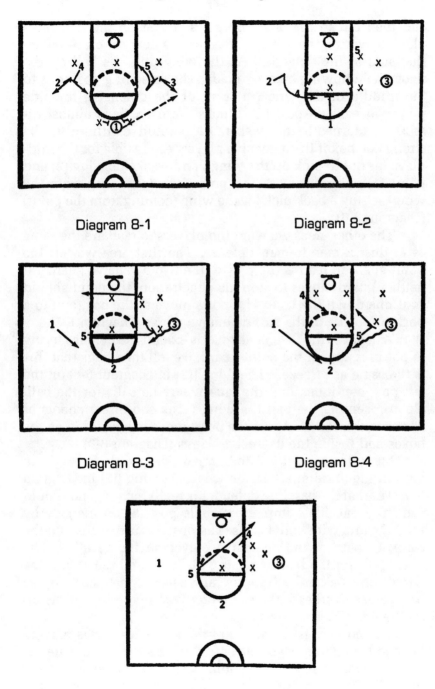

Diagram 8-1

Diagram 8-2

Diagram 8-3

Diagram 8-4

Diagram 8-5

and then out to the side and set a screen on the defensive player covering the wing. The screen is now set on the baseline side of the defender. As the wing puts the ball on the floor, the following cuts are made: The screening post rolls to the middle of the lane (in front of the defensive top-side player), weakside post (4) "ducks" into the lane almost directly underneath the basket, (he should continue to the strongside box if the defensive player responsible for the middle steps out to pick up the wing), and weakside wing (2) and point (1) exchange with the point (who's coming from the wing) setting a back pick for the wing (coming from the point) (Diagram 8-6).

The other areas we want the players to read are the same as against a man-to-man defense. The first area we tell the point guard to read is the play of the two defensive guards. If neither guard moves to stop his penetration, the point should continue down the lane. The posts move to the box, and to a position inside of the two defensive wings (Diagram 8-7).

Whenever the defensive guards extend the defense trying to put pressure on the point guard, we tell the wings that this is the same as "freeze." The wing [(2) in Diagram 8-8] on the left now continues into the lane where he calls for the ball. Upon receiving the ball the wing turns and either shoots or drives to the basket. Again the posts move to a position on the boxes and inside the defensive wings (Diagram 8-8).

Many teams will tell their weakside people to sag in to help in the middle. When the weakside wing [(2) in Diagram 8-9] sees that the baseline defender is really sagging, he should run the weakside bump. He signals post (5) on his side by pushing him with both hands. The post, in turn, steps into the recovery path of the defensive player on the baseline. The wing calls for the ball by raising his hand and the strongside wing throws a hard lob to the far corner of the court. As the ball passes overhead, the screening post pivots and posts up on the box (Diagram 8-9).

The posts must be aware of the defensive wings moving out and trying to prevent the entrance pass to the wing area. If this happens, the (4) man should flash up the lane calling for the ball. This is particularly effective when the opponent is

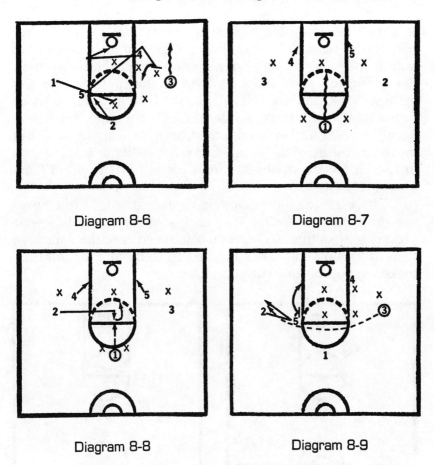

Diagram 8-6

Diagram 8-7

Diagram 8-8

Diagram 8-9

playing a spread type of zone, where the guards are out trying to harrass the point and the defensive wings have moved out to the wing area (Diagram 8-10). As far as the posts' positioning goes, we expect them to post up as if they are always in a man-to-man situation. Many players will not work for position against a zone, but by acting as if the defense is the same, they will find that they are still wide open when they face a zone, and in fact they will probably be even more open than with a man-to-man. The wing also must read this as if it were a man-to-man situation, looking for the hand as a signal as to where the post wants the ball passed.

The weakside post [(5) a Diagram 8-11] must also read the defensive position of the players on the strong side. When he sees that the strongside defensive guard is covering the wing with the ball and the weakside guard is sagging back into the middle, he treats this the same as if his man is helping out on the strongside post, and cuts hard to the high post on the ball-side (Diagram 8-11). If (5) gets the ball, he looks to shoot to low-post man (4), weakside wing {1) coming off a screen from the point [(2)], and then to strongside wing (3) who has moved to a seam of the zone—this will usually be a spot a step or two in toward the basket from his original position (Diagram 8-12).

These are the most common areas that will be open during the course of facing a zone. It's important to tell your players to treat this the same as before and read the defensive man in the area they are supposed to be cutting to, and then make the appropriate counter move.

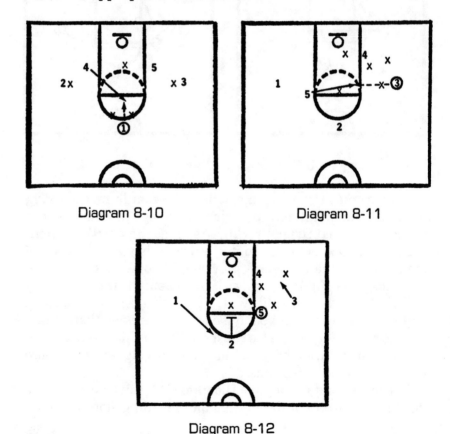

Diagram 8-10   Diagram 8-11

Diagram 8-12

The Calls vs. a 2–3 Zone

Some of the different calls will be discussed here to show how they would look against the 2–3 zone. The plays will work the same as they do against the man-to-man defense.

32. As the ball is passed to your (3) man, the post on that side clears to the weak side. The point guard cuts down the lane and also clears to the weak side, setting a triple screen for the weakside wing. The wing with the ball will now look for the weakside wing coming off the screen or the point guard who has stepped behind the screen of the two posts (Diagram 8-13).

13. As the point guard cuts through the lane, he continues to the corner on the ball-side. It is important that the point cut around behind the defensive wing, and not in front of him. This will allow him a moment to get the ball and shoot before the defensive man has an opportunity to recover to the area (Diagram 8-14).

23. Weakside wing (2) now cuts to the strongside corner, again around the defensive wing. As he moves past the defensive man he should get himself into a position to receive the ball and be able to go right up with it. The point guard starts his cut down the lane, but then pops back out to the top of the key (Diagram 8-15).

43. As the ball is passed to the wing, post man (4) steps out to the corner area. Diagram 8-16 shows what the call "43" looks like when (4) is on the same side as the initial pass. Note that as (4) steps out to the side, (5) now comes across the lane and down to the box. In Diagram 8-17, (4) is on the weak side and now comes across the lane low, behind the defense, and then out to the corner. In either case (4) should be in the "3" area and (5) ends up on the strongside box.

14. You can usually post up any player against a zone. Most teams will not deny tough when they are playing a zone defense—this includes the post area. We have found that by taking a player who posts up very well, he can usually get open in the zone. Just like against a man-to-man defense, the post on the side of the first pass always clears when the last number of the call is either "2" or "4." The point guard now comes down the lane and posts up on the box. The weakside

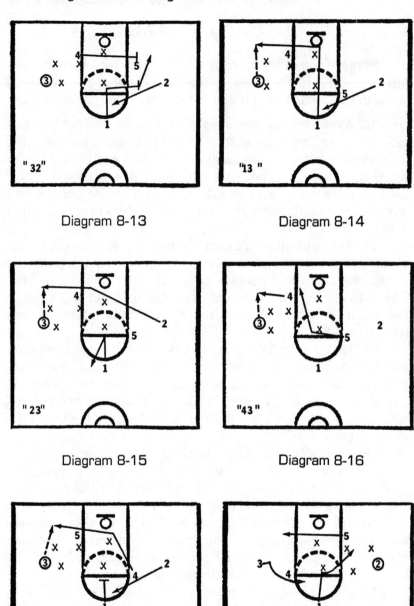

Diagram 8-13   Diagram 8-14

Diagram 8-15   Diagram 8-16

Diagram 8-17   Diagram 8-18

wing moves out to the top for defensive balance, and the weakside post stays high opposite the ball (Diagram 8-18).

15. One of the most effective plays we have found against the 2–3 zone is a lob pass into the lane. It is generally open more for the wings and point guard, because the defense is usually concentrating on stopping the post players from getting the ball. After (1) passes the ball to the wing, he should walk toward the weakside guard as before, then cut hard down the lane, right at the front of the basket. The wing should pass him the ball soon enough so that control may be gained (Diagram 8-19). The weakside wing moves out to the top for defensive balance.

30. Most zones are coached to move with the ball, shifting the entire zone toward the strong side. To take advantage of this, it is necessary to be able to throw the "skip" pass over the zone for better shots, and to force the defense to move more. The wing on the strongside, (2), holds the ball until weakside wing (3) moves behind a screen set by the weakside post. The post must move to a position where he is in between (3) and the defender responsible for the weakside coverage—this is usually the baseline defensive man (Diagram 8-20). Player (2) now passes the ball,using a hard lob pass to the opposite side. As soon as the ball passes over the head of the weakside post he should turn and post up on the box. Wing (3) has the option to shoot or to pass the ball inside or to hold it and run the offense from there.

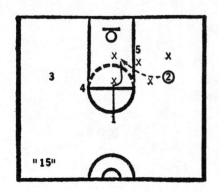

Diagram 8-19

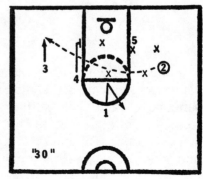

Diagram 8-20

Using the Screen and Roll
vs. the 2–3 Zone

One of the most effective calls we have against the zone is the screen and roll series. The plays that will be covered here will show some of the different variations you may like to try depending on your personnel.

131. The point guard calls for wing (3) to set a screen for him in the "1" area. The wing looks for the defender in that area and sets a pick on him as if he were covering the point guard one on one. As the guard drives by the screen, the wing now rolls to the box on that side; the post, who had cleared to the weak side, ducks in; the weakside wing moves out to the point; and the weakside post stays in the high-post area (Diagram 8-21).

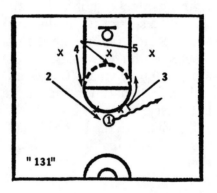

Diagram 8-21

252. The weakside post must always read which of the defenders is covering the wing area. If the wing with the ball is being covered by the free throw line defender, the post should come across high and set the screen on the top side of the defensive man (Diagram 8-22). On the other hand, if the baseline defender is covering the wing, the screen should be set on the baseline side (Diagram 8-23). In either case, as the wing drives past the screen, the rest of the players move as they did before. The weakside post ducks in, the player on the point moves to the wing area, and the player on the wing moves out to the point. The only difference is who sets the screen on the weak side. On the topside screen, the player on the point screens for the wing, while on the baseline screen, the player coming from the wing picks for the man who is now at the point. The post who screens always rolls away from the ball.

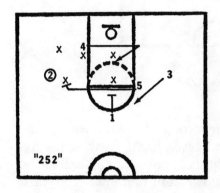

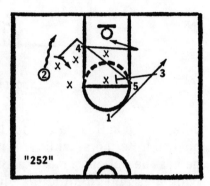

Diagram 8-22   Diagram 8-23

THE MULTIFLEX VS.
THE 1–3–1 ZONE

The only real difference in attacking any of the zones will be in your initial approach. After the ball is passed to the wing, all zones become the same as a 2–3, and from here will be attacked the same. What we will cover here is the basic way to begin attacking the zone.

The 1–3–1 has its weaknesses in the seams to the side of the defensive point, and to the sides of the baseline defender. The point guard is responsible for attacking the zone and drawing two defenders to him. As he penetrates to one side, the opposite wing [(2) in Diagram 8-24] must move into the seam on the opposite side. Weakside post (4) steps up into the recovery path of the defensive wing, trying to keep the defender on his back. Strongside post (5) is above the box on his side, and strongside wing (3) moves to an open area on the same side—this will usually be in the near corner (Diagram

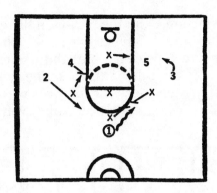

Diagram 8-24

8-24). If the ball is passed to the strongside wing, we run the offense from there, while if it is passed to the weakside wing, he has the option of either shooting, or driving the ball to the wing area and running the offense from that side. The most effective way of beating the 1–3–1 zone, though, is by getting the ball immediately to one of the post players. The weakside post will almost always be open if he does his job and steps up into the path of the wing on his side. By keeping this man away from the baseline area, there will be a natural passing lane open for a pass from the point (Diagram 8-25). The baseline defender is taught to move to the strong side of the zone as soon as the point guard commits himself (Diagram 8-25).

All of the other plays that were run before against the 2–3 zone will also work against the 1–3–1. The thing that you must teach your players is which defensive man to screen on the various calls, especially on the lob to the corner, the weakside post screening for the wing, and the screen for the point on the screen and roll.

30. On the lob to the weak side, post man (4) must get in the recovery path of the baseline defender—this is the defensive man who was on the wing in the initial setup (Diagram 8-26).

252. The post will always set the screen on the top side of the defense. The wing defender is the one responsible for that

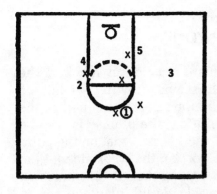

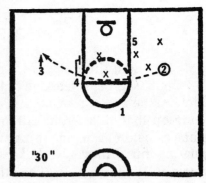

Diagram 8-25   Diagram 8-26

defensive area. As the wing drives off the screen, the only defender left to pick up the ball is the defensive point. This will leave the player coming off the weakside screen wide open for a shot at the free throw line (Diagram 8-27).

131. We run this play a little different than we did before. The wing now sets the screen on the wing defender and not the point guard. Unless that man is playing his position very wide, this will open up the entire side as the point drives by the screen. The rest of the offensive players move as they did before (Diagram 8-28).

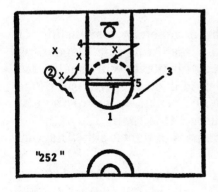

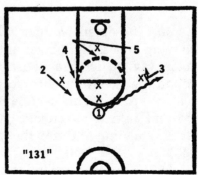

Diagram 8-27   Diagram 8-28

THE MULTIFLEX VS.
THE 3–2 ZONE

The main thing the point guard must do in attacking the 3–2 zone is to penetrate one of the seams, drawing two men to him. As he accomplishes this, he then passes the ball to the wing on that side. From this point on, the offense is run the same as before. The one thing we add here is that on the point guard's initial move, we tell the post on the weak side [(4)] to duck in (Diagram 8-29). The other thing that the players must learn is who to screen on any weakside lob play and screen and roll situations.

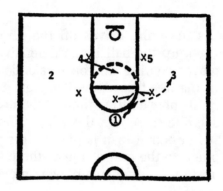

Diagram 8-29

30. The defensive man who is generally responsible for the wing area is the player at the free throw line. Depending on the way the defense is coached, this player will usually stay around the free throw line when he is on the weak side. The weakside post [(4) in Diagram 8-30] must now step up a step or two and into the recovery path of this man, allowing the strongside wing to throw the lob pass to the far side (Diagram 8-30).

252. As earlier, we tell the post to come across and set the screen on the wing defender. We tell the post, however, that the screen should always be set on the baseline side of the defender. This will force the defensive post to step out and help out, opening up the inside box area (Diagram 8-31).

131. As in the 1–3–1, we tell the wing to set the screen on the defensive wing and not on the defensive point. This play looks identical to the one we run against the 1–3–1 zone.

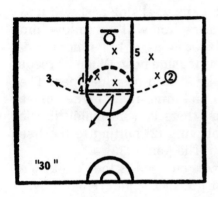

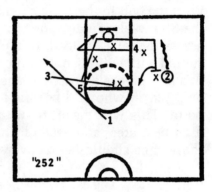

Diagram 8-30   Diagram 8-31

THE MULTIFLEX VS.
THE MATCH-UP ZONE

There are a wide variety of match-up zones, but all of them have the same basic principle: Pick up the offensive player in your area. Keeping this in mind you will find that the Multiflex Offense is an excellent counter to this defense. If the players read their keys, you will score with ease and consistency.

The match-up that we will use to demonstrate the offense's effectiveness is the 1–2–2 match-up zone. This most closely parallels the basic set of the Multiflex Offense.

The offense again starts with the wings exchanging sides as the point guard brings the ball into the front-court area. Because the defensive wings will automatically switch as they exchange, we tell the wings that they should look to "freeze" in the lane every time they cross. At some point in the lane the two defensive wings will back off, allowing the wing who is setting the screen in the lane to step up to the ball. (He should always call for the ball with his hands.) If he is open, the point should get him the ball in the lane, where he turns squaring himself to the basket. He has the option to shoot, drive to the basket, or dish off to either one of the posts (Diagram 8-32).

The next area that will usually be open is the weakside post [(4) in Diagram 8-33] on his flash move across the lane. With the ball in the wing's hands, the weakside post will find that the weakside defender covering him will not follow him across the lane. Instead, this player is going to be more concerned with helping out on the strongside post. When he reads this and breaks across the lane he should be wide open. The only player who will be able to pick him up is the defensive point. This will mean, first, that there is a mismatch in the high-post area, and second, that wing (2) cutting to the free throw area should be uncovered (Diagram 8-33).

The last regular area that will be open is the "continuation" series. The weakside post [(5) in Diagram 8-34] moves across to the strongside where he sets a screen for wing (2) with the ball. As the wing drives past the screen, the defense is now forced to rotate to pick up the player with the ball. This in turn will free one of the other offensive players, who make the same cuts as we have already discussed (Diagram 8-34). It should be noted here that this particular play against this particular defense will open up the strongside power layup for the wing. The defense is very slow to move in this direction, thus freeing the player with the ball for this move.

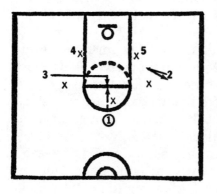

Diagram 8-32

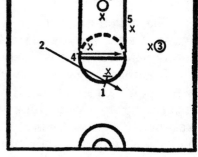

Diagram 8-33

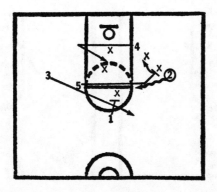

Diagram 8-34

THE CALLS AGAINST
THE MATCH-UP ZONE

Sometimes you will find that the match-up defense lends itself to using our call system more than against other defenses. There is a certain amount of inflexibility we have found in the match-up zone, so that calling a certain play will take advantage of this situation.

15. As the point guard begins to cut down the lane, the defensive point and wing will now switch. The point now breaks hard down the lane looking for a return pass from the wing. It is important that the wing gets the ball to the point a little quicker than we normally would when we run this play, because the weakside defensive post will usually be sagging off in the lane to prevent any penetrating passes near the basket (Diagram 8-35).

25. Like "15," the switch that automatically takes place will free the wing who now breaks backdoor instead of out to the free throw line area. He should be sure to make his cut in front of the post defender as he moves to the basket (Diagram 8-36).

43. Every one of the "3" series calls will work here because the defense will be so used to your team running a balanced floor, that they will be slow to cover as any of the

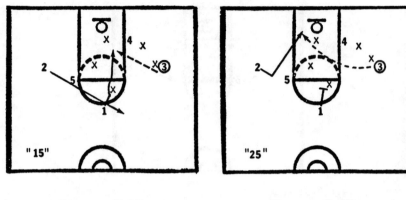

Diagram 8-35   Diagram 8-36

players move to the corner on the strongside. The post steps out to the corner to get the ball, and the opposite post now fills in, moving to the box on the strongside. This play works best when the post has to come across the lane to the corner (Diagram 8-37), although it is still very effective run either way.

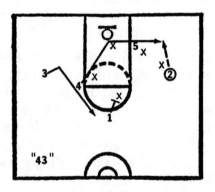

Diagram 8-37

30. Like all defenses, the players in the match-up are told to sag toward the ball to help out. This makes any play where the skip pass is thrown very effective. As (2) receives the ball, (3) moves to an open position on the weak side, at the same time the weakside post steps into the recovery path of the defender. (This will be the defensive man who started off on the wing near the free throw line.) When (3) receives the ball he has the same options as before: Shoot, hit the post rolling to the basket, or run the offense from here (Diagram 8-38).

By running the offense, looking for the keys, and by occasionally making some of the suggested calls, you will find that the match-up zone is a very easy defense to score against. Like everything else, it is best to drill your team against this type of defense so they feel comfortable when they see it in a game.

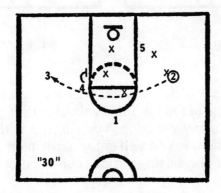

Diagram 8-38

THE MULTIFLEX VS.
THE 1–2–2 ZONE

The 1–2–2 zone is attacked much the same as the 3–2 zone. The main difference here is that the weakside defensive wing is more likely to move to the baseline once the ball is passed to the strongside wing. This will mean that the screens will be set more to the baseline side on all cross-court lob plays, but will still be on the baseline side on all screen and roll plays on the wing. Diagram 8-39 shows what "30" will look like against the 1–2–2 zone, and Diagram 8-40 is the way "252" should look like against this same defense.

We have covered just some of the different plays or calls that can be made against each of the defenses. To describe each one would take a whole book in itself. You may find that from year to year, depending on the personnel you have avail-

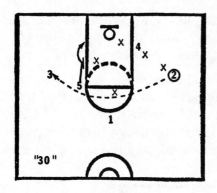

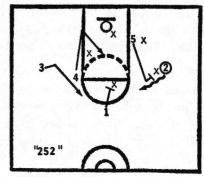

Diagram 8-39   Diagram 8-40

able to you, that different calls will work better sometimes than others. One of the fun things about running the Multiflex Offense is the many variations you can run without changing the basic set offense. You will enjoy experimenting with some of the different plays using various combinations of players to run them.

9

The Multiflex Offense vs. Combination Defenses

There may be times in a season where an opponent will try combination defenses to stop one or two of your top scorers. The Multiflex Offense does not have to be altered to beat this type of situation. By using the main offensive pattern, cuts and screens, it will open up scoring opportunities not only for the players not getting the special attention, but also for your top offensive people the defense is designed to neutralize. This chapter will deal with some of the calls that you may want to try against these defenses, as well as to show how using the basic cuts and being patient open up all sorts of scoring opportunities.

THE BASIC CUTS AND SCREENS VS. THE BOX AND ONE

The wings exchange as the point guard drives his man into the top of the free throw circle. The posts again screen for the wings as they exchange as before. The player who has drawn the special coverage should now be the recipient of all screens. (If your players are unable to recognize who is getting the one-on-one coverage, it doesn't matter, because eventually that player will get open anyway.) As the wings cross, the posts now turn and screen again. As is evident by the following series of diagrams, the defender covering your top player is now running through a series of screens and will find it very difficult to stay with his man. Diagrams 9-1 through 9-3 show how the Multiflex Offense looks against the box and one defense.

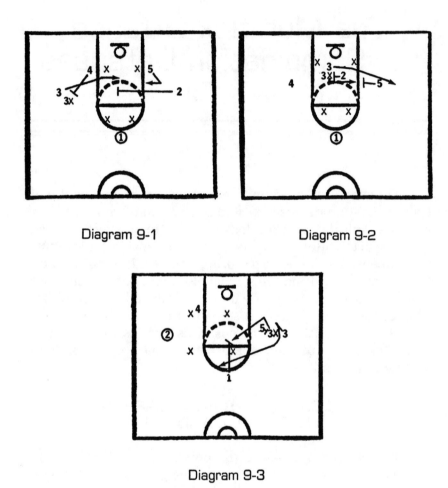

Diagram 9-1   Diagram 9-2

Diagram 9-3

The Calls vs. the Box and One

Some of the calls we have found to be effective against the box and one defense will be described here. It should be noted that we really don't do anything special or different in running our offense to counter the box. We may make certain calls depending on the player receiving the special coverage, but again all the calls are plays that we have available to us at all times.

35. It is assumed here that the player the opponent has decided to deny the ball is our (3) man. The rest of the calls will center around freeing this player. It should be noted that these same calls will work equally well for both (1) and (2), and on occasion for (4) and (5). As the ball is passed to strongside wing (2) our (3) player should take his defender a step or two toward the top of the key. He then cuts hard to the basket using the screens set for him by both the weakside post and (1). Player (2) should throw the ball so that (3) has plenty of time to react to it, gain control, and score (Diagram 9-4).

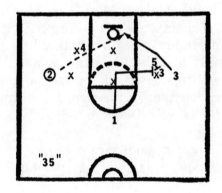

Diagram 9-4

30. Even though (3) is receiving special attention, the rest of the players will still sag toward the strong side. (On occasion so will the player covering (3).) We tell (3) to run this play in a similar fashion to the way we run "bump." Player (3) should take his man in as if he were cutting to the free throw line, then push the weakside post, signaling him to turn and screen his man. Although the post may not be able to get in between (3) and his man, he still should be able to set a screen so that (3) can either back off, or move to the corner. The ball is then thrown by (2) on a hard lob crosscourt to (3) who should be open (Diagram 9-5).

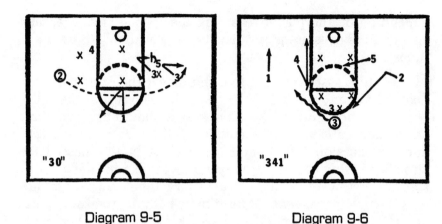

Diagram 9-5   Diagram 9-6

341. This particular play is set up by having (3) come out to the top for a handoff by (1). After he gets the ball, (4) should move up and set a screen for (3). We prefer that (4) set the screen on the defender in the free throw line area. It is now (3)'s responsibility to drive his man down and then into the area that (4) is setting the screen. If done properly, (4) will not only screen the defender in the free throw line area but the man covering (3) as well (Diagram 9-6).

THE MULTIFLEX VS.
THE DIAMOND AND ONE

Like the box and one, the diamond will place one individual on your best player, trying to take him out of the offense. The main difference here is in the alignment of the remaining defensive people. There will now be a defensive player out on the point, two defenders even with the free throw line, and the last player under the basket. The best way to attack this defense is to have the point guard penetrate into a seam, drawing two defenders to him, then passing the ball to one of the open players. Similar to the 1–3–1, we want the post opposite the penetration to step up to the ball, pinning the defensive wing man on his back. It should be mentioned that we will always exchange the wings to begin the offense so that the defensive man is run through the whole series of screens.

If the ball is passed to one of the wings, we run the offense from there (Diagram 9-7). Ideally, what we want to see happen is (1) being able to hit one of the posts who will then take the ball up and score.

Some of the different reads that should be open against this defense are the freeze move by the wing not being covered, the fade or curl move by the wing being covered, the weakside post flashing to the strong side, and the weakside bump. Diagrams 9-8 through 9-12 will cover each of these reads respectively.

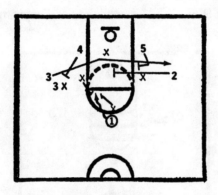

Diagram 9-7

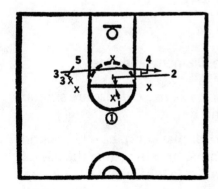

Diagram 9-8

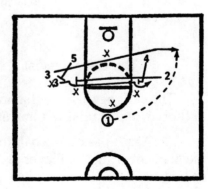

Diagram 9-9

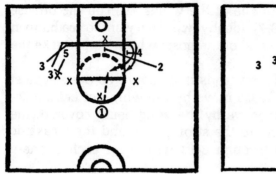 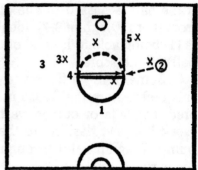

Diagram 9-10   Diagram 9-11

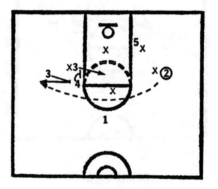

Diagram 9-12

The Calls against the Diamond and One

The calls against the diamond and one defense are similar to those used against the box and one.

35. As (1) passes the ball to our player (2), he cuts around the man covering (3). Player (3) must time his cut to the basket so that his man is now picked off by (1). As he makes his cut, player (2) should try to get the ball to him as soon as he is open in the lane. After (3) makes his move to the basket, (1) should back out to the top of the key (Diagram 9-13).

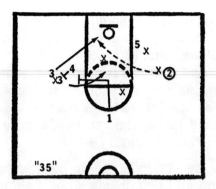

Diagram 9-13

30. When the ball is on the opposite side of the wing being covered one on one, we can usually run our lob play to the weak side. Again (3) should "bump" the post on his side, then move back out to either the side or the corner, depending on where the post is able to set the screen (Diagram 9-14).

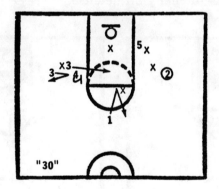

Diagram 9-14

342. It may be necessary to run through the basic pattern two or three times in order to get the ball to (3) on the wing. The other way to do this is to have (3) come out to the point and receive the ball from (1) by way of a handoff, and then have (3) dribble the ball to the wing area. When (3) has the ball

on the wing, post player (4) should step out and set a screen for (3). The post, however, should set the screen on the defensive wing in that area, and (3) must then drive the man covering him into the screen. If this is properly executed, (3) will be able to run both his man and the defensive wing into (4)'s screen. We prefer that (4) set the screen on the baseline side (Diagram 9-15), but he has the option of also setting it on the top side of the defense (Diagram 9-16).

These calls are very effective in countering the box and one and diamond and one defenses but it should be emphasized here that the most effective way of countering these defenses is simply to run the basic cuts and screens. The defender who stays with your top player through the multiple screens will have to be a very unique individual.

One more item of interest, a second way to counter these types of defenses is to have the player being covered one on one take the ball and drive his man into screens, and in turn get the defensive player in foul trouble. This will only work once or twice, but may just be enough to cause the defender to lose some of his intensity on defense.

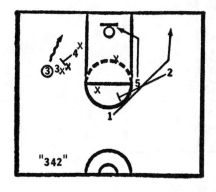

Diagram 9-15

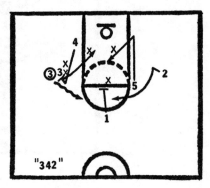

Diagram 9-16

THE MULTIFLEX VS.
THE TRIANGLE AND TWO

You may on occasion run into a team who is trying to deny the ball to two of your better ball players. In this situation you may find that by simply running the basic offense, with its series of cuts and screens, you will be able to free one or both of these players on a regular basis. The following diagrams—9-17 through 9-20 will show what the offense will look like against the triangle and two defense. In these diagrams we will assume that (1) and (2) are the players drawing the special attention.

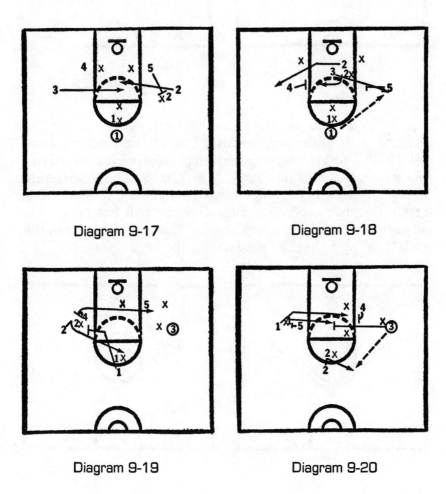

Diagram 9-17

Diagram 9-18

Diagram 9-19

Diagram 9-20

As in the box and one, the same set of plays will work equally well against the triangle and two. Diagram 9-21 shows what a play like "15" will look like, while diagram 9-22 demonstrates our "20" call.

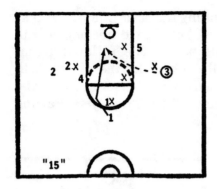

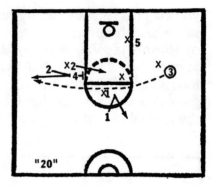

Diagram 9-21   Diagram 9-22

You can also use the screen and roll series against this defense with great effectiveness. One of the most effective calls in this series is having the two players being covered run the screen and roll, such as in "121," or "212." By screening for each other you can often force a switch and in most cases create confusion, because most coaches will not cover this situation in their pregame planning. Diagram 9-23 shows the call "121" and Diagram 9-24 covers the "212" play.

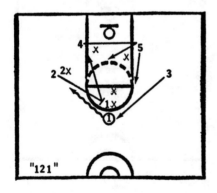

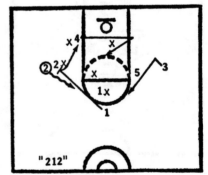

Diagram 9-23   Diagram 9-24

No matter what defense you run up against it is important that your players try to run the basic offensive pattern. This will be your most effective weapon against any defense. The second thing they must keep in mind is to read the defense. If they watch the players in the area they are supposed to be cutting to and respond accordingly, they will find themselves open no matter what the defense.

By using the basic cuts and supplementing the offense with the calls, you will be in control of any situation that may arise. You may want to experiment during the course of the season in practice against some of these different defenses simply to give your team confidence if they should happen to face them at some point.

10

The Fast Break
into the Multiflex Offense

Every coach has his own feelings about the type of tempo he wants to have his team play. Some prefer to control the ball and run a very disciplined, slow-down game. Others race up and down the floor as fast as they can. We prefer to get the ball out on the break but keep it under control. By running the fast break we feel that it gets us easy baskets and puts extra pressure on our opponent's defense.

The Multiflex Offense lends itself very well to any of the above styles of play. What will be discussed here is the specific break we run and how we move from this break right into the Multiflex set.

The break that we use is a designated break, and although this break is a little slower developing than just filling the lanes, we feel it does have some distinct advantages. The designated break is more consistent, each player has specific responsibilities, and most important, it gets the ball into the hands of our best ballhandler and passer, and that means fewer turnovers.

THE THREE-MAN BREAK

We run every time we get the ball; after a rebound, after a steal, and even after a made free throw or basket. In the course of this chapter we will explain each. The most common break is the three-man break after a rebound.

As the shot is taken the (2) man releases down the floor, always heading directly toward the basket. The only time he doesn't release is when the man he is covering on defense is closer than 15 feet to the basket. In this case he must first screen out his man, and when he sees that the ball is rebounding into another area, he releases as before. Player (1) moves to the side the ball is rebounded. He should try to get some depth. We prefer that he be beyond the top of the circle and somewhere from the center of the court to within three feet of the sideline. Player (3) fills the far lane, the one away from the rebound, getting wide as soon as possible. He should be in his lane by the time he has reached half court. The post who doesn't rebound [(5) in Diagram 10-1] moves slightly opposite the ball and hesitates at the near free throw line in case the outlet passer needs a safety valve (Diagram 10-1).

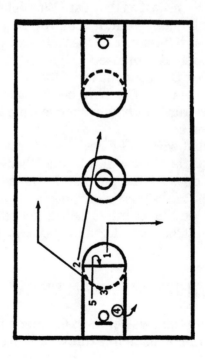

Diagram 10-1

The player who rebounds the ball should follow our number one rule, look to shoot. This will force him to turn and look up-court for player (2), who has released. The pivot we want him to make is a front, or forward, pivot, on the foot nearest to the sideline that he is nearest. Ideally, we would like him to pull the ball down and start to turn on his way back down to the floor. The ball should remain at face level with the elbows spread. The forward pivot to the outside will help prevent the defense from "jamming" the rebounder and hindering him in throwing the outlet.

The rebounder throws the ball long to (2) only if he is wide open (Diagram 10-2). If player (2) is not open, the rebounder now looks for (1). When (1) receives the ball, his first move is the same as the rebounder—pivot and look up-court. If player (1) sees that (2) is open, he may pass the ball ahead. Player (2) should now be standing under our basket. If (2) is still not

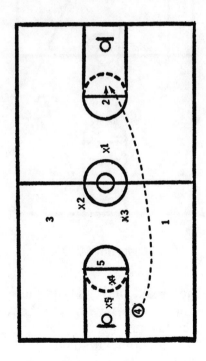

Diagram 10-2

open, (1) brings the ball up the court with the dribble, driving directly at the near corner of the free throw line. Player (2) sees that (3) is able to get out on the break so he now moves to the wing area on the same side as the ball. Player (3), who is in the far lane, goes hard, then angles to the box when he gets to the free throw line extended. The post who did not rebound the ball is the first trailer and goes down the side opposite the ball and even with the lane. The rebounder is the second trailer and goes down the court in the outside lane on the side of the ball (Diagram 10-3).

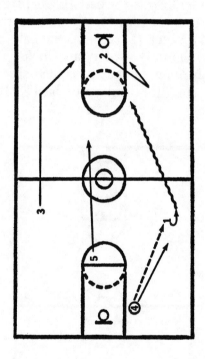

Diagram 10-3

As we run the break, player (1) is the quarterback who will direct where the ball goes, who is to shoot, and even what kind of shot is to be taken.

Whenever (1) passes the ball ahead to (2) from a position near half court, (2) is expected to take the ball to the basket.

Player (2) will only be passed the ball when (1) sees that there is an advantage. This means that (2) will either be all alone, or that he is in a position to beat the defensive man who is back (Diagram 10-4).

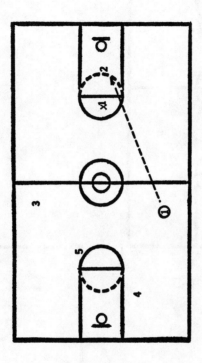

Diagram 10-4

When (1) brings the ball up the court on the dribble, he must determine if either of the wings is open and for what kind of shot. If (1) feels that (2) or (3) have an open lane to the basket for a lay-up he will throw a bounce pass to the open player (Diagram 10-5).

If (1) feels that (2) or (3) are open for the jumper, he now throws a chest pass (Diagram 10-6). We insist that on all jumpers off the break, every player on the wing shoot the ball off the glass. It is essential that the wings come at the basket in a straight line from the free throw line extended. Don't let them "banana" (Diagram 10-7).

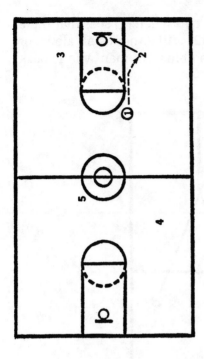

Diagram 10-5

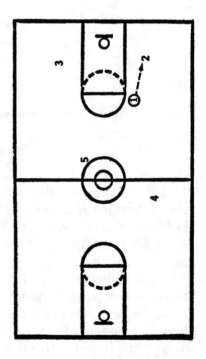

Diagram 10-6

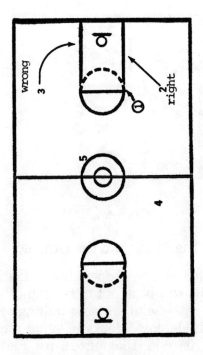

Diagram 10-7

Player (1) has the option to take the ball to the basket if the defenders are split and not set in tandem (Diagram 10-8). He also has the option of pulling up and taking the jumper if the defense is playing him soft (Diagram 10-9).

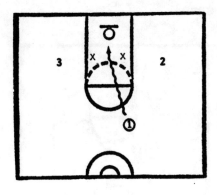

Diagram 10-8

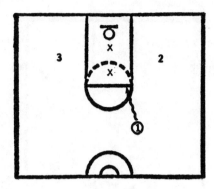

Diagram 10-9

The Break into the Offense

If (1) feels that no one is open during the first part of the break he pulls the ball back out to the top of the key. At the same time both posts, who are now trailing set picks for the wings. The weakside post "ducks in" after setting the screen for the wing on his side (Diagram 10-10). Player (1) looks to the post inside, then to the wings. If the ball is passed to the wing, you now run the regular Multiflex Offense (Diagram 10-11). But if no one is open, the wings exchange as described in the first chapter and we start the offense without having to really stop and set things up (Diagram 10-12). This keeps additional pressure on the defense because it doesn't allow them to matchup the way they want unless they switch, which may leave someone open.

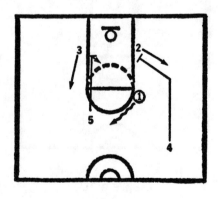

Diagram 10-10

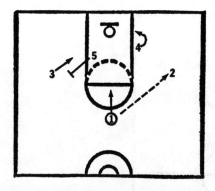

Diagram 10-11

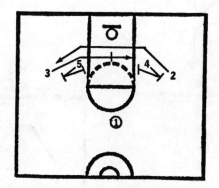

Diagram 10-12

If player (1) is not open on the initial outlet, the rebounder should now look for (3) on the far side. If the ball is passed to (3), he pivots and looks for (1) who makes a diagonal cut across the floor toward the ball. If (1) is open, (3) passes him the ball. From here the break is virtually the same as before with the following adjustments: The trailer on the ball-side has to get wide, and the second trailer now comes down even with the lane (Diagram 10-13).

If player (1) still isn't open, (3) takes the ball down the court. As he gets to the free throw line extended, he now drives the ball toward the basket. Player (1) still breaks to the elbow and the trailers come down as described before (Diagram 10-14).

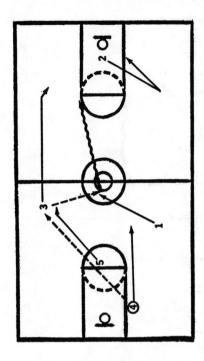

Diagram 10-13

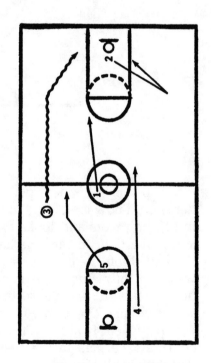

Diagram 10-14

If either (1), (2), or (3) gets the rebound, they have the option of bringing the ball up the court on the dribble to start the break or of getting the ball to (1). Whenever they bring the ball up themselves they should take it up the near sideline. Player (1) will fill the middle and the other wing the far lane. We want (1) in the middle of *all* breaks (Diagram 10-15).

Diagrams 10-16, 10-17, and 10-18 show what the break looks like on the opposite side.

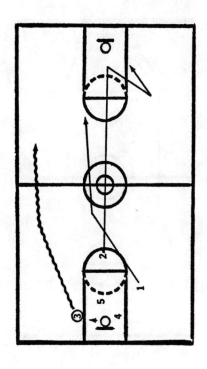

Diagram 10-15

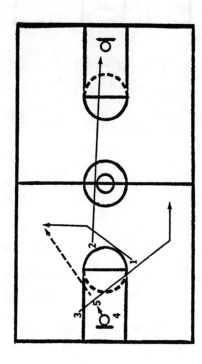

Diagram 10-16

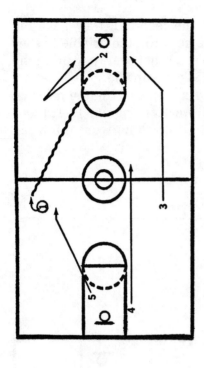

Diagram 10-17

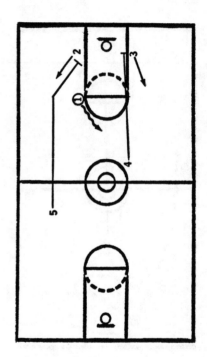

Diagram 10-18

The Three-Man Break
Following a Field Goal

When our opponents score we want to put immediate pressure on their defense. The key to running the break from here is to get the ball in quickly and to push the ball up the court. Either (4) or (5) takes the ball out of bounds. There are two very important techniques involved here for the posts. First, whoever takes the ball out must run out of bounds—he cannot walk or jog; he must sprint. Second, as this player is sprinting out of bounds, he must already be looking downcourt. By looking over his shoulder, the post can see if (2) is going to be open on the release or if the pass should be thrown to (1) in the outlet area. Just as in the three-man break after a missed field goal, (2) has released long, (1) has moved to the side of the ball, and (3) has started down the far lane (Diagram 10-19). The break is run just as before, with (1), (2), and (3) in the lanes, while (4) and (5) trail in their respective lanes (Diagram 10-20).

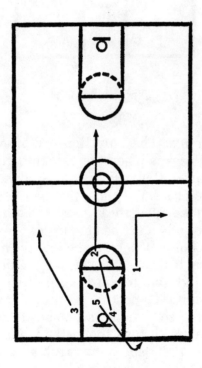

Diagram 10-19

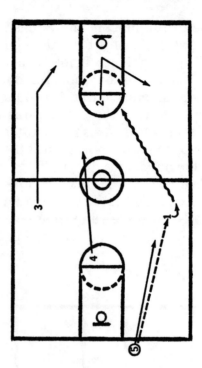

Diagram 10-20

Coaching Points. The only time we allow (4) or (5) to throw a baseball pass is when they are throwing the ball the length of the court—otherwise they must always throw some sort of two-handed pass. We prefer that they get in the habit of throwing a two-handed overhead pass. Also, the player throwing the ball in bounds must be able to see the whole court at once. In fact, he should be looking behind the man he is thinking of passing the ball to, so he can see if a defensive man is sneaking up behind him, trying to steal the pass.

Coaching Point. The post taking the ball out must always clear the lane area so that he is not positioned behind the backboard when he throws the ball in bounds. Diagrams 10-21, 10-22, and 10-23 show the break after a made basket. We will only run the three-man break after a basket. If (3) can't get out on the break after a made basket, then he isn't trying, and should be replaced by someone who will try.

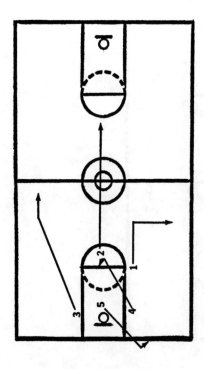

Diagram 10-21

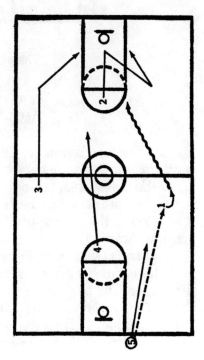

Diagram 10-22

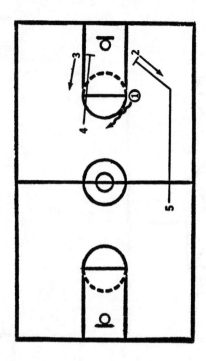

Diagram 10-23

THE TWO-MAN BREAK

As before, our number (2) man will release on the shot. He positions himself under the basket. After the ball is thrown to (1) in the outlet area, (2) looks up-court to see if (3) has gotten out on the break. When he is unable to fill the third lane, (2) must step to the side opposite (1). This signals to (1) that we are now running the two-man break (Diagram 10-24).

When (1) sees that player (2) has moved to the weak side, he flattens out his drive downcourt so that he is now heading directly for the box on his side. As player (1) reaches the free throw line extended, we want him to make a hesitation or stutter dribble. This stutter dribble will keep the point guard under control, and at the same time force the defensive man back to commit to one player or the other. Any defensive fakes that he may use will now be useless.

As (3) finally gets out, he must now take the middle position on the break. He always cuts to the corner of the free throw line on the side of the ball (Diagram 10-25). Players (4) and (5) trail as before, with the trailer on the side of the ball filling the outside lane and the trailer opposite the ball coming down even with the lane (Diagram 10-26).

If (1) or (2) doesn't have a shot, the ball is passed back out to (3). Player (3) waits for the posts to set the down picks just as in the three-man break. Everything from here is virtually the same. Player (3) looks for the posts rolling off the screens, then the players breaking out to the wings. Diagrams 10-27 and 10-28 show the offense after the two-man break.

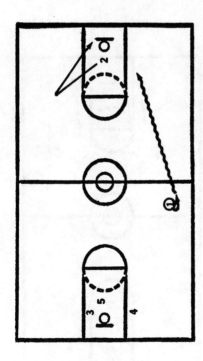

Diagram 10-24

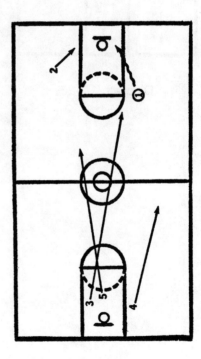

Diagram 10-25

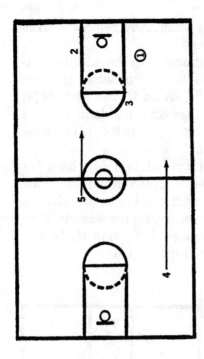

Diagram 10-26

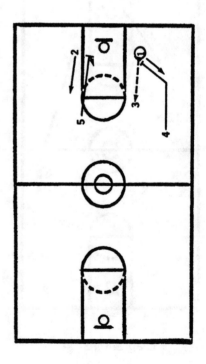

Diagram 10-27

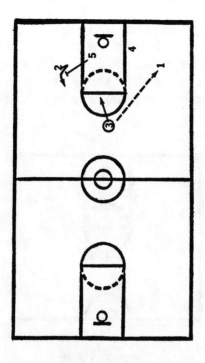

Diagram 10-28

BREAKING AFTER FREE THROWS

We try to break every time we get the ball. This holds true even when our opponents are shooting free throws. We line up the same way each time. Players (4) and (5) take the first spot on each side of the lane. We will usually take our best rebounder of those two players and put him on the same side of the lane as our opponent's best rebounder. Players (2) and (3) will take the third position on the lane and the point guard stands above the top of the circle (Diagram 10-29). Players (4) and (5) must step in and screen out their men. We teach our players to put all of their weight on their foot closest to the baseline. This will enable them to be able to step into the lane quicker. They must make contact with their men, then ride them out. Players (2) and (3) are responsible for any opponent on the lane further from the basket than they are. If there is a man there they must screen him out with the same move that the posts use. If there are no players next to them on the lane they now must screen out the shooter (Diagram 10-30). All players on the lane must have their hands above their shoulders, to prevent the man next to them from hooking their arm and stopping them from jumping.

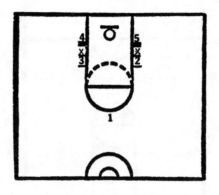

Diagram 10-29

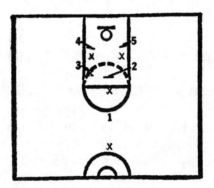

Diagram 10-30

If the shot is missed, player (1) moves to the side the ball is rebounded, while (2), after screening out his man or the shooter, releases down the middle of the court, and (3) fills the far lane. As you can see, these are exactly the same positions that the players are in when we run the break after a missed basket. Players (4) and (5) trail just as in the other break (Diagrams 10-31 and 10-32).

If the free throw is made, either (4) or (5) takes the ball out of bounds, with the other man moving to the free throw line. Player (1) breaks to the side the ball is being inbounded, (2) releases long, and (3) fills the far outside lane (Diagram 10-33). From here the break is exactly the same as the three-man break from a missed field goal.

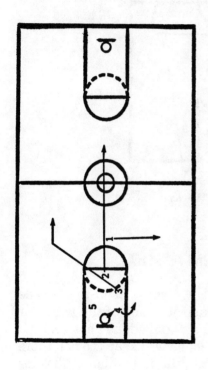

Diagram 10-31

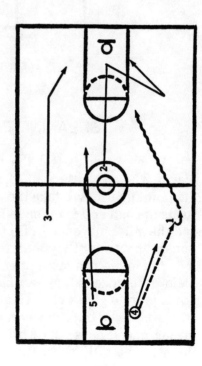

Diagram 10-32

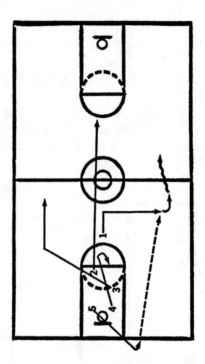

Diagram 10-33

BREAKING FROM A STEAL

Whenever we steal the ball, we run a lane break. The player who steals the ball, provided it is one of the wings or the point guard, will take the ball down the lane he is in. If he steals the ball and is in the left lane, he will keep the ball there and the other players will fill the middle and far lane. All rules remain the same (Diagrams 10-34 and 10-35).

Again we can run either a two- or three-man break. The main difference is that because of the steal we won't have (2) downcourt to give a visual signal to determine which break we are going to be in. The key now is a verbal call by the man in the far lane. If he is out by himself with the man who has made the steal he will yell "two." But if he sees that there is a

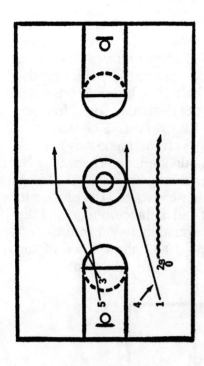

Diagram 10-34

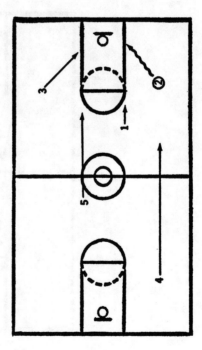

Diagram 10-35

teammate in the middle he will now yell "three." Diagram
10-36 shows what the break may look like if we can get only
two men out, while Diagram 10-37 shows what a three-man
break may look like after a steal. If one of the posts gets the
steal we want him to outlet the ball as if he got a rebound.
Unlike the regular break, we will not designate lanes. Instead,
we tell the players to get out and fill the lanes. The player on
the side of the steal looks for the pass from the post, while the
other players fill the middle and outside lane. There may be
times in this break that (4) and (5) actually get out on the break
and fill one of the lanes. In this situation we tell the players to
break, keeping the proper spacing and distance, and to end the
break by being in a position to immediately get into the offense. Diagrams 10-38, 10-39, and 10-40 show three of the
different possibilities that may arise in this situation.

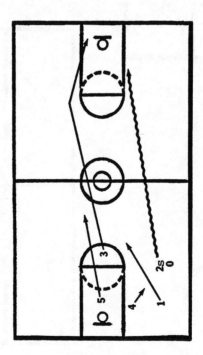

Diagram 10-36

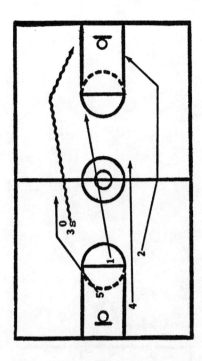

Diagram 10-37

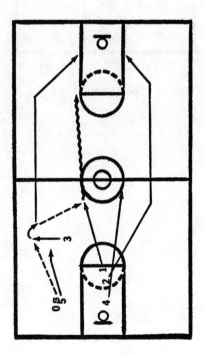

Diagram 10-38

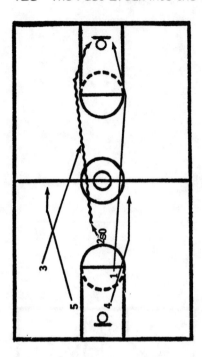

Diagram 10-39

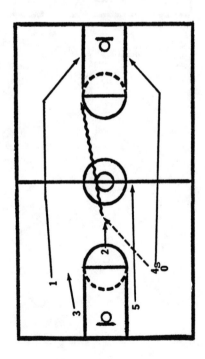

Diagram 10-40

COUNTERS TO THE DEFENSIVE OVERPLAY

After running the break a number of times, the opponents may try to take away some of the things you are doing. The following pages will cover the most common defensive adjustments and the ways to counter them.

The first thing most defenses will try to take away is the outlet pass to the point guard. When this happens, there are two things you can do to counter. First, the point guard should step into the defender and call for the ball with the hand away from the defender. The post who is taking the ball out of bounds must look to see if there is another defensive man in the area. If there isn't, he now passes the ball over the defense. The point guard does not release to catch the ball until it is directly over his head. Once he gets the ball, we should definitely have an advantage and should score off of either the two- or three-man break (Diagrams 10-41 and 10-42).

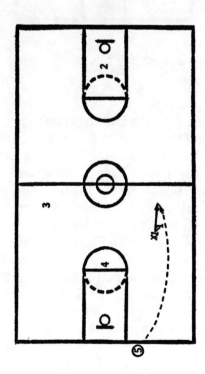

Diagram 10-41

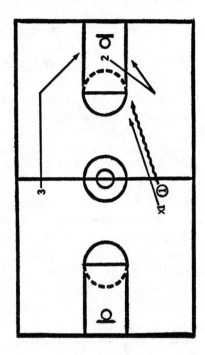

Diagram 10-42

If the post can't get the ball to (1) on the counter move, he will now try to get the ball into the other post who is posting up at the free throw line. As the ball is thrown into the post [(4) in Diagram 10-43], (1), who has posted up as described before, now pivots on the foot closest to his man and pins him on his hip. He now cuts diagonally across the court. The post at the free throw line [(4)] pivots and looks up-court. He first looks to (2), then to (1), and then to (3). The other post comes in on the same side he was on and acts as a safety valve if no one else is open. Eventually, when the ball is passed to either (1) or (3), the players turn and take the ball up the court with the break the same as before. The only difference is that the ball will now be on the opposite side of the floor (Diagram 10-43).

In the event that the post at the free throw line cannot get the ball to either (1), (2), or (3), he now passes the ball back to the other post. He then moves to the next circle and posts up again. Players (1) and (3) will maintain their positions on their respective sides and (2) will stay active underneath (Diagram 10-44).

If the ball is passed to (3), either from the post out of bounds or the post at the free throw line, he pivots and looks up court to (2). Player (1) then cuts diagonally across the court. If (1) is open, (3) should pass him the ball. If he's not open, (3) then takes the ball up the sideline, and (1) continues down the center of the court toward the corner of the free throw line (Diagram 10-45). The key to breaking the defensive adjustments is to move the ball to the middle and then to the opposite side of the court. The players must also keep moving, but within the framework of the regular break.

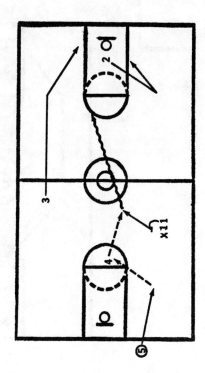

Diagram 10-43

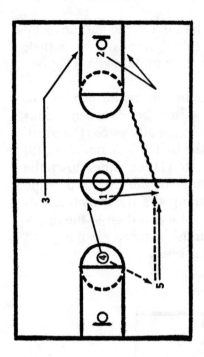

Diagram 10-44

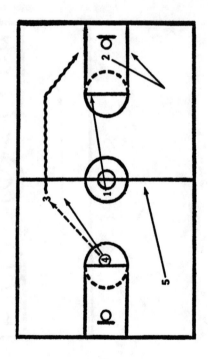

Diagram 10-45

ALTERNATE BREAKS

There may be times when it will be to your advantage to use some type of alternate break. The two breaks we have found to be most successful will be described here.

Whenever we want to change the break we call out a code word or number. This can be anything that your team can easily remember. The first thing we do is change the responsibilities of the release man, (2), and the point guard, (1). In this case, (1) becomes the release man and (2) becomes the outlet. The rest of the break and responsibilities remain the same for each of the respective break positions. Player (1) is on the wing and (2) becomes the point (Diagram 10-46). The offense at the end of this is the same as before except that (1) starts off on the wing and (2) begins on the point (Diagram 10-47 and 10-48).

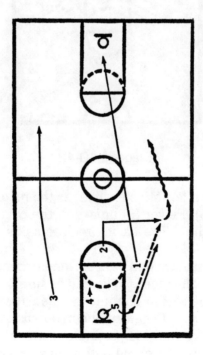

Diagram 10-46

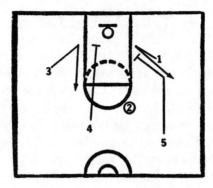

Diagram 10-47

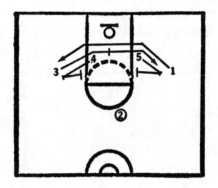

Diagram 10-48

The second alternative exchanges the responsibilities between (1) and (3). Player (3) breaks to the outlet area and (1) fills the far sideline. The basic break remains the same (Diagram 10-49).

As you can see, we don't get extremely complicated in the alternate breaks. The idea is to keep it as simple as possible but to still have some sort of counter to defensive pressure.

One further note to getting the ball in as quickly as possible. Since we have run this particular break after a made basket we have had little trouble with teams pressing us in some sort of zone trap. They simply don't have enough time to set

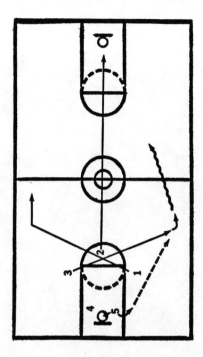

Diagram 10-49

up the way they want. There are teams that will try to press us man to man, but these situations will be covered in a later chapter.

To sum up this chapter, try to break whenever you can, after every shot, made or missed. You'll like this system because it puts additional pressure on your opponent's defense, you'll be able to get many easy baskets, and it can be very demoralizing to your opponents.

One thing you as the coach must do is be patient with your players when they first start to run the break. At first there will be a rash of mistakes and turnovers. But with patience and practice these mistakes will decrease and the benefits will be tremendous.

11

Using the Multiflex Break as the Press Offense

BREAKING AFTER A BASKET

We have found that by breaking after both missed and made baskets, that we are able to beat most presses before they are able to get set up. The key here is the same as in the break after a made basket. The post taking the ball out must sprint out of bounds (outside the lane area), looking over his shoulder as he does so. He first looks long to our release man. This option is particularly effective against the teams that try to zone press. Teams that use some sort of zone pressure will usually put their big man back under the basket to prevent any lay-ups. This player, however, has to run the length of the floor to get into position. This means that this player is not going to be in position to stop the long pass to your (2) man (Diagram 11-1).

If the release man isn't open the post then looks to our point guard near the 28-foot marker. Again the point guard uses the same technique. He should get deep enough on the side of the ball and cut toward the sideline. If he is overplayed by a defender, he should try to hook the defender and call for the ball long. This last move is particularly effective against man-to-man defenses. If the ball is thrown into the point he pivots, looking up-court to (2). If (2) is open, he then passes him the ball. If (2) isn't open, (1) now drives the ball to the near

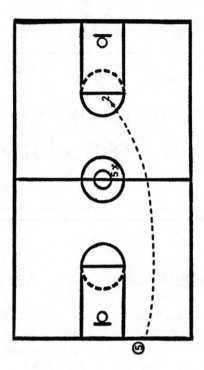

Diagram 11-1

corner of the free throw line. It is important that (2) cut back out toward the ball if he is not open long. If the defense is zone pressing, this move will usually free him, or at least give (1) another outlet pass (Diagram 11-2).

The (3) man releases up the side, opposite the post taking the ball out of bounds. He should try to get wide as soon as possible, keeping his eye on the ball at all times. The post will look to this player as his third option on the in bounds pass, with (3) being ready to come back and meet the ball if necessary. If the ball is passed to (3) initially, he pivots to the middle and looks for (1) coming across the court toward the ball. If (1) is open, (3) should get him the ball, and then continue down the outside lane toward the basket (Diagram 11-3).

If player (1) isn't open, (3) keeps the ball and dribbles down the court staying in the outside lane, with (1) continuing down the center to a spot at the corner of the free throw line.

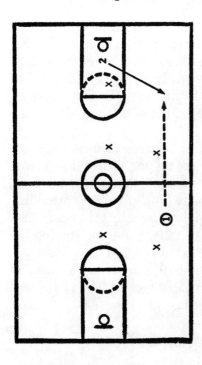

Diagram 11-2

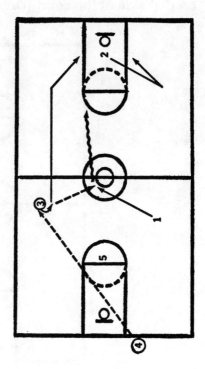

Diagram 11-3

As (3) hits the free throw line extended he should try to turn the corner and take the ball to the basket for a lay-up. The better defensive teams will take this move away from the wing, so his second option is to simply keep the ball on the wing and wait for the trailers, (4) and (5). He also has the option of getting the ball back to (1) in the middle anytime that (1) is free.

The post not taking the ball out moves to a position at your opponent's free throw line. Here he posts up and calls for the ball. If all the other players are covered, this post is our last option. If the ball is thrown to him, he must pivot up-court and look for the open man. At the same time we tell (1) to cut to the middle of the floor, (3) to step back to the ball while staying in the outside lane, and (2) to cut to the side (this is the same side as before). After the post passes the ball in bounds, he should step in on the near side of the court, in effect taking (1)'s place on that side of the court (Diagram 11-4).

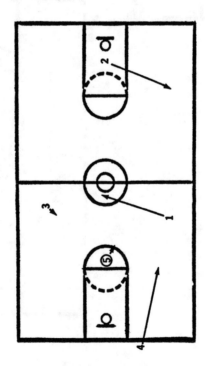

Diagram 11-4

From here we run the break according to who the post passes the ball to. If the ball goes to either (1), (2), or (3) we run the break as we have already described. If the ball is passed back to the other post, who has stepped in bounds, (1) must now break back to that side. He should try to get a little depth on his cut so that your team will always be moving the ball up-court, attacking the press and your opponents' basket. The post at the free throw line must also move up-court. We tell him to move to the next circle and post up again (Diagram 11-5).

There are a couple of things we stress to the players when they face a press. First, always come and meet all passes. Second, be patient, but aggressive. We want to make our opponent pay for trying to press us. We also tell our players that they should be able to determine if the press is man-to-man or zone. Against the man-to-man press we simply get the ball to one of our better ball handlers, preferably our point guard, and

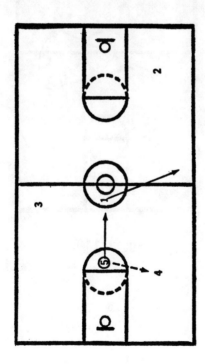

Diagram 11-5

tell him to bring the ball up, with the rest of the players clearing to the other end. We tell the point to try to bring the ball up
the middle of the floor. His teammates must be alert for the
teams that like to run and jump on the press. When this situation occurs, we tell the player whose defender is running to
the trap to cut behind it to the side opposite his initial position
(Diagram 11-6). We do this to screw up the rotation of the help
defense.

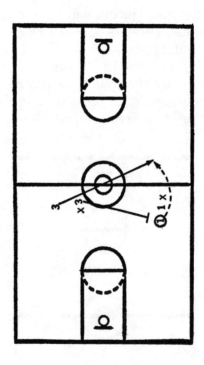

Diagram 11-6

Diagrams 11-7 and 11-8 show what the offense looks like against a man-to-man press.

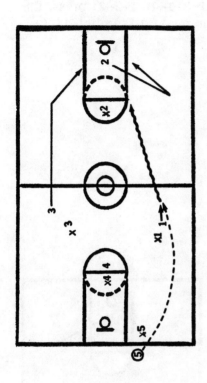

Diagram 11-7

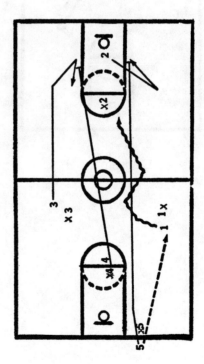

Diagram 11-8

Diagram 11-9 shows how the offense should look against the team that uses the man-to-man, run-and-jump press.

Against teams that use the 1–2–1–1 (1–2–2) press, the offense should look like this (Diagrams 11-10 through 11-12).

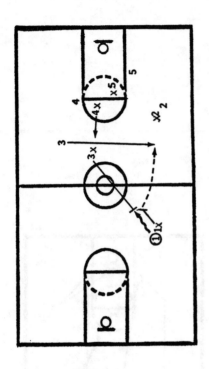

Diagram 11-9

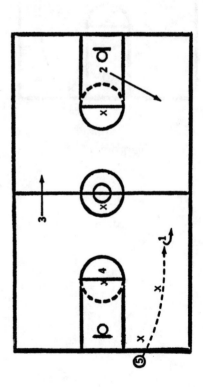

Diagram 11-10

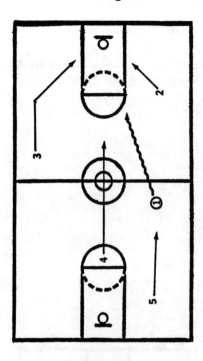

Diagram 11-11

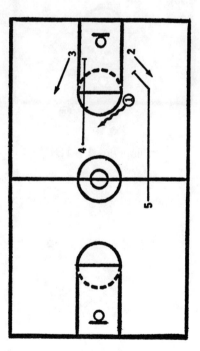

Diagram 11-12

Diagrams 11-13 through 11-15 demonstrate what the offense will look like against the 2–2–1 zone press.

In all cases it is important to remind the post that the first option is always the release man long, provided he is open.

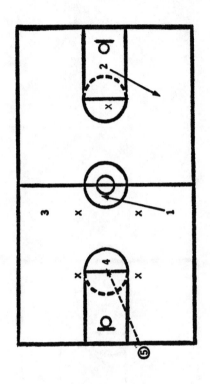

Diagram 11-13

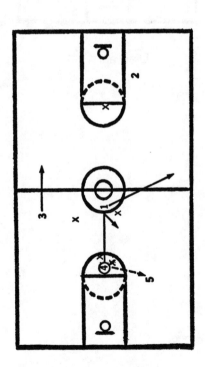

Diagram 11-14

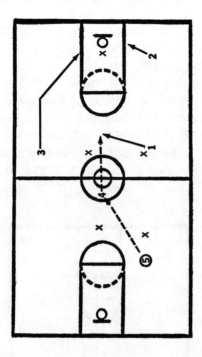

Diagram 11-15

BREAKING AFTER
A SUCCESSFUL FREE THROW

We break the same after a successful free throw as we do after a basket. We align ourselves the same way as described in Chapter 10. The only difference here may be the side we take the ball out. Generally speaking, most players are right-handed and will then take the ball out on the right side of the basket. To give us more flexibility and to be less predictable, we will occasionally have the post take the ball out to the left. We will signal this a number of ways, by using either a preset number or color. This will signify not only what player we want to take the ball out but on which side. For example, we may designate that we want our (4) player to take the ball out simply by calling his number. His rule is to always take the ball out opposite the side he lines up on the free throw lane.

All of our players now know that if the free throw is made we will be running the break to the side opposite (4)'s original position (Diagram 11-16).

The call for this will be made by the point guard after getting the call from the bench. It should be noted that although your players should be encouraged to take the ball out on both sides, that during game situations, you will usually find that they take the ball out more to one side than the other. The free throw situation gives you a chance to balance this out some more.

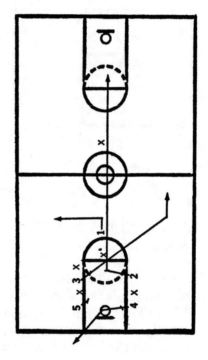

Diagram 11-16

OUT-OF-BOUNDS ENDLINE BREAK

When there is a violation, it gives the opponent the opportunity to set up their press. We don't feel this presents any special problem for the Multiflex Offense. We align the players in the order shown here. The point guard, (1), lines up behind the center of the free throw line. Player (2) is right behind him; (3) is next, and (4) and (5) are last in line. It is best, in this situation, to have your post who is the best passer take the ball out and use the other one as the last person in the stack. As the referee hands the ball to the post, the players break. Player (1) curls around (2) and (3) then cuts to the same side the ball is on, and approximately even with the 28-foot marker. As player (1) passes him, (2) also releases, curling away from the ball and toward our basket. The post player at the end of the stack is responsible for head hunting (2)'s man. Player (3) breaks to the far side, then turns and starts up the sideline, always keeping his eye on the ball. After (5) screens for the release man he steps up to the free throw line and posts up (Diagram 11-17).

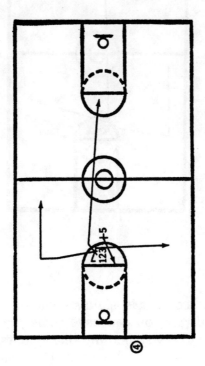

Diagram 11-17

The options are the same as before—(2) long, (1) at the 28-foot marker, (3) on the far side, and the remaining post at the free throw line.

The counters discussed in Chapter 10 are also very useful here. The first counter is signaled by the point guard who taps (2) on the leg. This tap signifies that (1) and (2) are to switch responsibilities, with (1) going long and (2) breaking out to the 28-foot marker. In either case though, (1) will always break first (Diagram 11-18).

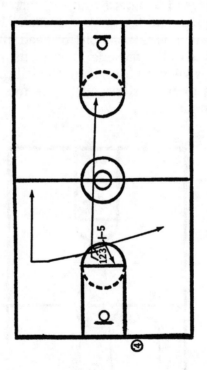

Diagram 11-18

The second counter is again signaled by (1). We tell him to turn and tell (3). You can have some prearranged call or simply tell him to say something like, "yours." As the ball is handed to the player out of bounds, (1) breaks out to the far side, (2) goes long, and (3) cuts to the 28-foot marker on the side of the ball (Diagram 11-19).

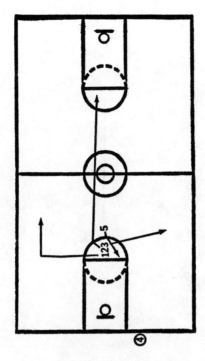

Diagram 11-19

OUT-OF-BOUNDS SIDELINE BREAK

After some violations, the ball will be taken out on the side. We align ourselves the same way as before, except that the players are now side by side facing the sideline. Player (1) is first, followed by (2), (3), and the remaining post player. From here everything is exactly the same as before. Player (1) curls around (2) and (3), then moves to the side of the ball. Player (2) curls behind everyone, then releases long, (3) breaks opposite the release man, and then to the far sideline, and the post—after head hunting (2)'s man—posts up trying to get the ball. The one coaching point to stress here is to make sure that the players don't align themselves too close to the ball initially. We prefer that they stay in line with the near free throw lane (Diagram 11-20).

This press offense has been very good to us. In fact, there

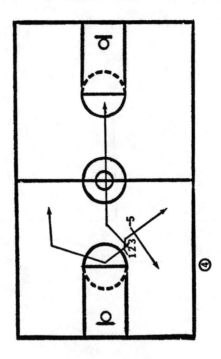

Diagram 11-20

are very few teams that have ever pressed us for any length of time. We are usually able to score out of this press offense, making it impractical for our opponents to keep pressing us. Along the same lines we have found that because we break after successful free throws and baskets, that most teams are more concerned about getting back to defend the break than about being able to press us.

Furthermore, although the press offense seems rather simple, by executing it and taking advantage of the counters, you will find that even the best defensive teams will not be able to stop your team from scoring off the press offense, because you are actually scoring off your break. You will also find that your players will develop a lot of confidence in this offense, both as a break and as a press offense, because they don't have to learn a number of different offenses to run against the various presses they will see in the course of the season.

12

How the Multiflex
Lends Itself
to Special Situations

THE MULTIFLEX AS A
HALF-COURT-PRESS OFFENSE

Some teams will throw a half-court press against you to disrupt your team's offensive flow. Again, the best way to beat this is to get downcourt before they have a chance to set up. This is particularly effective after a missed or made basket or free throw, because most of the players are not in an immediate position to get back if you get the ball up quickly.

There are times, however, that you will not be able to beat the opponent up the court, especially after a violation.

We attack all half-court traps the same way. We tell the point guard to first call, "half-court." The rest of the players must respond immediately to this call. From here the two wings break out immediately to the side they're on, cutting to a position above the top of the free throw circle. Players (4) and (5) also move out to the side, moving about four to five feet away from the lane.

The point guard now penetrates between the two trap men, drawing both of them to him. As the defenders move in to trap the point, he passes the ball to one of the wings [(2) in Diagram 12-1]. The point guard now cuts between the defenders looking for a return pass from the wing. The other wing

[(3)] stays in an open seam of the defense. This will usually be the corner directly across from the first pass, but on occasion he may have to cut to the middle of the court (Diagram 12-1).

When the point guard gets the ball back he should square up to the basket and try to penetrate, just as he would in "point." The posts stay wide until (1) penetrates to the basket. At that time they cut to the box on their side, looking for a pass from (1) (Diagram 12-2).

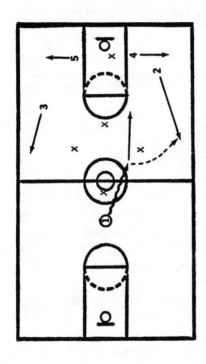

Diagram 12-1

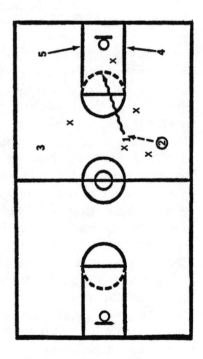

Diagram 12-2

There will be times when the defense will try to prevent you from passing the ball back to (1). In this case, or if the defense is slow moving over to trap the wing with the ball, wing (2) now has the option of taking the ball to the basket himself. Again, the posts move to the boxes as the wing penetrates (Diagram 12-3).

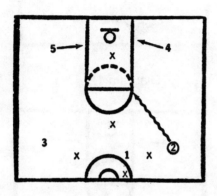

Diagram 12-3

We run this offense against any half-court-trap defense. The following diagrams will demonstrate how it will look against the most common half-court defenses. Diagrams 12-4 and 12-5 show the half-court offense versus the 1–3–1 trap. (This is probably the most common defensive half-court trap you will see.) Diagrams 12-6 and 12-7 cover the offense against the 2–1–2 half-court trap. Diagrams 12-8 and 12-9 show what the offense will look like against the 2–2–1 zone trap.

This offense is very similar to the "four corners" offense used by so many teams. The major difference here is that we will always try to score out of this offense. We feel that the best way to get the other team to call off the press is to make them pay for using it in the first place. By telling the players to run this as if it were our "point" offense they know exactly what we want them to do, and at the same time, we haven't given them another offense to remember. We will show you in the next section how we also use this as part of our control game.

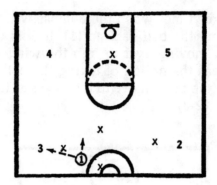

Diagram 12-4

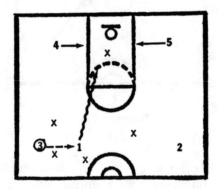

Diagram 12-5

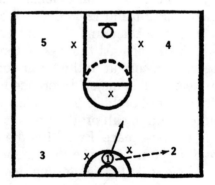

Diagram 12-6

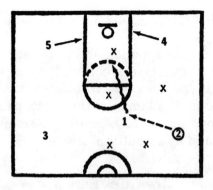

Diagram 12-7

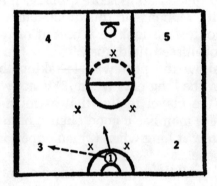

Diagram 12-8

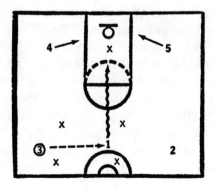

Diagram 12-9

CONTROLLING THE TEMPO

Depending on the situation and opponent, you may find that you will want your team to control the tempo of the game. This section will show you how you can use the Multiflex Offense to speed up the tempo of the game, or slow it down. We will also cover using the offense as a semidelay game, a spread offense, and as an outright freeze.

The Quick Series

When you find yourself behind late in the game and you need to pick up the tempo to score quickly, it is very easy to adapt the Multiflex Offense to this quick-tempo style of play. The players should first look to score off of the break, after either a made or missed field goal. This is the one time you may want to allow the post who is taking the ball out of bounds to throw the long pass when (2) is not wide open. It is important that the player realize that he must only throw it long if the release man has a good chance of getting the ball. To rush and throw it long when (2) isn't open is just going to defeat the purpose.

If the break isn't there, we want the players to get the ball to the wing position, and then if possible into the post. We tell the players to take the first open shot they have *within* their range. If the wing has the ball and he cannot get the ball into the post, we then want him to try to drive the ball to the basket using a crossover move to the baseline. When we are in our quick series we tell the players not to cut after the first pass. The post on the weak side stays there, as does the wing. The point guard remains on the point (Diagrams 12-10 and 12-11).

Coaching Point: It is important that the players are still playing under control. Be quick, but don't hurry. As a coach it is necessary for you to make them understand that by rushing or forcing their shots, they are doing more harm than good. There are a couple of drills that we use to teach them this that will be covered in Chapter 13.

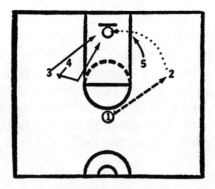

Diagram 12-10

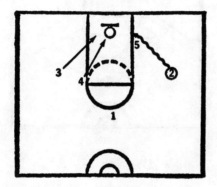

Diagram 12-11

Taking Time off the Clock

When we are in a situation where we are ahead and want to hold the ball, but are still looking to score, we run our "take time off the clock game." The offense is the same as we always run, except that we now will run it a little wider. The wings still exchange off the posts, but now they break out further. The point guard and wing exchange, as do the posts, (although we don't really look for this option as we do in the regular offense). The idea here is to get the clock down to the next minute digit. In other words, if the clock shows 4:35, the players know that they are not supposed to score until the clock reaches the 3:59 mark. The only shot we allow during this time is an uncontested lay-up. Once we have reached the next minute mark we go back into our regular offense, running it closer to the basket. The players may now shoot provided they have a good shot within their range. Diagrams 12-12 and 12-13 show what the "take time off the clock" offense looks like.

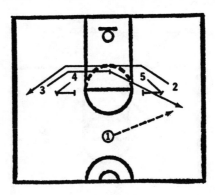

Diagram 12-12

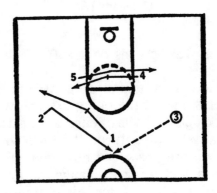

Diagram 12-13

Freeze

When we are in a position that we want to hold the ball completely, we run "freeze." This tells the players that there are to be *no* shots taken. They must realize at this point that the only opponent we have is the clock. We now have the wings take a position near the 28-foot marker, the posts step out to the corner, and the point guard has the ball in the middle. The point guard's job is to keep the ball from the defense, and when he is forced to give it up, he is then responsible for getting it back from the player he passed it to. This is similar to the four corners offense. Player (1) should always be within one pass of the ball. The other players stay in their respective areas, trying to stay in the open seams of the defense (Diagram 12-14).

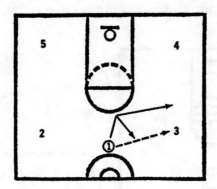

Diagram 12-14

Delay

The reason the "delay" offense is mentioned last is because we have had so much luck with our "time off the clock" offense that we seldom ever run this. For those coaches that like to have an offense in between the "time off the clock" and the "freeze," the Multiflex Offense lends itself well to this type of game. All we do here is run the "freeze" offense, but now we tell the players to look to score. If the point guard or either of the wings has an opening to the basket, they should penetrate to the basket with their dribble. As they do this, the posts now break to the boxes looking for a possible pass from the player penetrating. If nothing is open, the ball is brought back out front and the offense is run again (Diagrams 12-15 and 12-16).

By practicing the various situations that will arise in games, your players will become familiar with what you expect from them. They will also become familiar with the limitations. One thing of interest—you may want to consider the "time off the clock offense" as part of your game plan against the really strong teams that have you overmatched in talent. By reducing the game down to minutes instead of seconds between shots, you may find that your team is in a position to win the game in the final minutes or seconds.

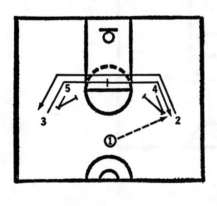

Diagram 12-15

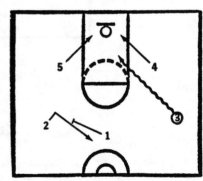

Diagram 12-16

OFFENSIVE REBOUNDING

An added advantage of using the Multiflex Offense is that the positioning in the offense assures you of being in good offensive rebounding position on all shots. In fact, we have found that a high percentage of our scoring comes off of second and third shots. Of course, like everything else in the offense, we work at rebounding. This section is designed to make you more aware of the offensive rebounding possibilities.

Positioning

Whenever a shot is attempted, we tell the posts that they must always go to the boards, with each of them taking one side of the basket: the weakside post on the weak side and the strongside post on the strong side. Even if the weakside post [(4) in Diagram 12-17] is on his way across the lane when the shot goes up, he must stop and get into rebounding position on the weak side (Diagram 12-17).

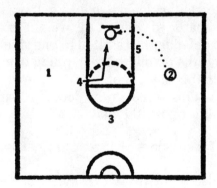

Diagram 12-17

Once the posts have switched sides they become responsible for the rebound position on their new side of the court (Diagram 12-18).

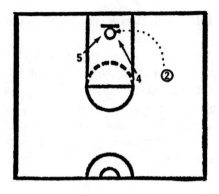

Diagram 12-18

The strongside post should try to roll off his man and into the lane. We want him to swing his foot away from the defender, and try to hook the defensive man on his back. At the same time, the post should bring his arms up so that the elbows are at shoulder height, and the hands even with his head. The weakside post, on the other hand, should cut to the basket, aiming for a position to the front and side of the rim. He should try to get the defensive man responsible for screening him off the boards to commit his weight to one side or the other. Once the defender has shifted to one side, the post must now step around the defender by stepping over the defensive man's foot with his near foot. At the same time, the post should try to hook his arm over the defender's arm, preventing him from jumping up for the ball.

Three and a Half on the Boards

We will also send the weakside offensive man to the boards on all shots. His positioning will depend on our game plan for each opponent. Before the game we will tell the players if we want 3 and a half or 2 and a half men on the boards. When we face a team that has less talent than we have or that doesn't run a particularly effective break, we send 3 and a half men to the glass. In this situation, the offensive player who is on the weakside wing at the time of the shot must get to a rebounding position on the weak side of the basket. We prefer that the wing take a position just inside of the weakside post. It is more important, however, that he just get to the boards. He uses much the same technique as the weakside post did to get inside position on his man. The half position we refer to is the strongside wing. As the ball is shot, we want this player to get to a position near the middle of the floor, around the broken circle. If there are any long rebounds, this player should be able to get to them from there. Diagram 12-19 shows the rebounding positions when we send three and a half to the glass.

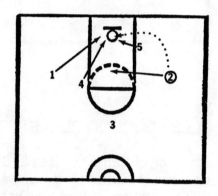

Diagram 12-19

Two and a Half on the Boards

When we come up against an opponent that has either far superior talent or an excellent fast break, we usually choose to send two and a half to the boards. In this case the posts still crash the boards, but now the weakside wing takes the rebounding position near the broken circle, while the strongside wing moves immediately to a defensive position along with the player now on the point (Diagram 12-20).

We feel it is very important that there always be some attempt to get any missed shots. The number of second and third shots your team is able to get often determines how you do in the won/lost column. Again, this phase of the game must be worked on and emphasized. Never underestimate its importance.

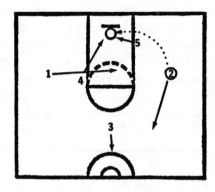

Diagram 12-20

LAST-SECOND PLAYS

There are a number of things we like to do in the final seconds of a game when the score is tied or we are down by one or two points. This section will set up some of the different situations and some of the plays we run off of our regular offense.

Full-Court Last-Second Plays

If we have the ball and have to go the length of the court to score, we have a number of options open to us. First, if there is enough time left on the clock (four or more seconds), we will not even call time out to set something up. Instead, we will run our regular break after a made basket. This will usually catch most teams sleeping. If a team scores against you with little time left on the clock they will expect you to call time, and will probably be so excited that they scored that they won't get back to cover on defense as they normally would.

The second thing we like to do is set up one of two special plays if there are less than four seconds left. The first play we call is "home run." The post who normally sets up as the last man in our stack positions himself on the broken circle under our basket. Players (1), (2), and (3) line up as before, but a little further downcourt. As the referee begins to hand the ball to our player out-of-bounds, these three break toward our basket, staying in the lanes they normally occupy. Players (2) and (3) are in the outside lanes and (1) is in the middle. The ball is thrown the length of the court to the post under our basket. (It helps if this player tells the referee that he's going to be fouled on the play. This at least alerts the official to watch the players on that end of the court instead of the flight of the ball.) If the post can catch the ball he does, then powers the ball up for a lay-up. If he can't get a clear shot at catching the ball, he should tip it to one of his teammates coming down in their various lanes (Diagram 12-21).

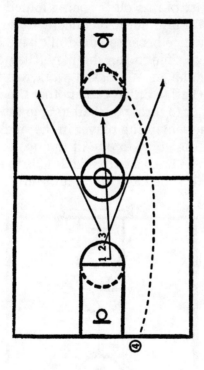

Diagram 12-21

Another play we like to use is very effective but only against certain teams. In order for this play to work, you need an opponent that places one man on your out-of-bounds man. When this happens we run "suicide." We start off the same way as we do in "home run," but now, as the referee begins to hand the ball to our player, we have one of our other players run out-of-bounds under our opponent's basket. When he has gotten out-of-bounds the post passes him the ball, then breaks quickly onto the court. As all this is going on we have another player in the stack (our best free throw shooter) come up behind the defender guarding the post, and set a blind pick. It is important that the screen be set one step behind the defensive man. As the defender turns to cover the post who is quickly moving in bounds, he will run into the screener, who then falls down. We want this player to make a loud sound, as if he was just hit by a truck. Of course, we have alerted the official as to the possibility of this player being fouled so that he will be more aware of it and not just concentrate on the ball. This play is especially nice because you don't have to worry about not having enough time to run the play (Diagram 12-22).

If this particular move doesn't work, we tell the player who now has the ball to either call another time out (provided we have one left) or to throw the ball long to the far post on the broken circle. The remaining player in the stack has broken to the other end of the court to one of the open areas. He must talk to the post as he breaks so that he is able to know where he should tip the ball if he can't catch it cleanly.

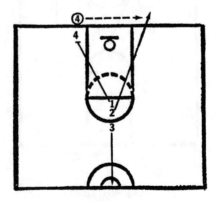

Diagram 12-22

Half-Court Last-Second Plays

If we have enough time and a number of time-outs left, we will get the ball to half court and then call time. We can do this right out of our regular offensive break after a made basket or after a time-out. All we are looking for here is the chance to get the ball closer to the basket for a last-second shot. The player taking the ball out-of-bounds must be aware of all the players on the court. The one exception to our regular offense that we make here is that (2) is told to come back to the ball in the middle after going long. This gives the inbounding player one more person to hit at half court. Once we get the ball to one of the players at half court everyone calls "time out."

Double Pick. There are several plays we like to run. The first we call "double pick." We line up with our best passer taking the ball out-of-bounds (usually our point guard, but not always). Player (2) (your best shooter) starts opposite the ball in the wing area. Player (5) is on the box on the strong side, (4) is at the high post on the opposite corner of the free throw line, and (3) is in the corner next to (5). As the ball is handed to (1), player (2) breaks across the lane toward the basket and then curls around the screen set by (5), and finally off of the screen set by (3). (Against man-to-man defense, (3) screens (2)'s man, while against a zone he simply walks into the baseline defender.) Player (4) has the option of either stepping to the ball or breaking down the lane, depending on how his man is playing him. We prefer that he set his man up so that he can go backdoor for a lob pass from the point guard (Diagram 12-23).

Step. We start "step" with the same alignment as we do on "double pick." The difference is that now (2) breaks out high off (4)'s screen and (3) steps in and sets a screen for (5) who cuts to the corner. As (5) steps out to the corner, (4) breaks down the lane, and (3) moves up the lane crossing with (4). Player (2) now sets a screen for (3) at the free throw line. Player (1) has the option of hitting (5) in the corner (he has the option then of either shooting or hitting (4) cutting to the basket) or passing to player (2) off (4)'s screen, or hitting (3) coming off the double screen of (4) and (2). Diagram 12-24 shows what this play looks like against man-to-man defense, while Diagram

12-25 demonstrates what it will look like versus a zone defense.

These plays have proven to be quite successful for us. They are plays that are run off of our regular offense and fit in nicely with our basic philosophy of offense. The next chapter will go into more detail as to how we actually practice these different situations so that the players are familiar with what we want to do in a given situation.

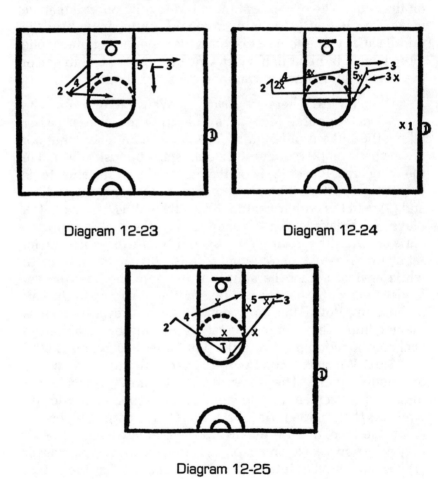

Diagram 12-23   Diagram 12-24

Diagram 12-25

13

Drills to Teach
the Multiflex Offense

This chapter is devoted to the drills we use for teaching the Multiflex Offense. These drills will be broken down into four different areas: teaching the offense (including the shooting drills we use), the break, the press offense, and controlling the tempo of the game.

TEACHING THE OFFENSE

The "Whole" Offense

We usually start by showing the players the whole offense starting from the break. We initially walk them through the entire sequence of moves and screens. By showing them the entire picture, we feel they have a better understanding of what we are trying to accomplish in each of the following drills:

Spot Shooting. The players start in two lines as shown in Diagram 13-1. Whenever possible we like each player to have his own ball. (If this isn't possible, we simply use what's available and have the players pass the ball to the next player in line as they approach that line.) Starting at half court, the player takes two dribbles toward the basket. We want the last dribble to come up hard to the shooting hand, that is, the right hand of all right-handed shooters and the left hand of all left-

handed shooters. The players should always start out dribbling with the hand closest to the outside of the court. (Right
hand on the right side, left hand on the left side.) As the ball
comes up to the shooting hand, the player should get himself
into a shooting position: knees bent, feet shoulder width apart,
head up. This will allow the player to go right up with the ball
off of the dribble. Too many times shooters will catch the ball
with their legs straight. They then have to bend their knees
before they shoot, allowing the defense to recover. After the
player shoots (it's important that the player goes up and comes
down in the same spot on each shot), he should follow his shot
and get his own rebound. He then continues, dribbling with
his outside hand, to the end of the opposite line (Diagram
13-1).

After the players have shot two times from each side of
the court (four shots each), the players then form a line at the
wing with the first player facing the basket. The remaining
players line up facing the players on offense, with the first
player in line acting as if he is playing defense (Diagram 13-2).
The offensive man uses a jab step and drives hard to the middle of the court. Again he uses two dribbles before he shoots.
The ball should be dribbled with the hand away from the
defender, but again the last dribble should come up hard to the
shooting hand after the second dribble. As the ball comes up
to this hand, the player should square up to the basket and

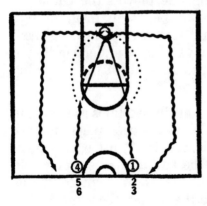

Diagram 13-1

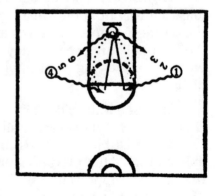

Diagram 13-2

shoot. After shooting, the player retrieves his shot and dribbles to the end of the opposite line, keeping the ball in his
outside hand. As soon as the first player has driven past the
"defender," the defender steps out to the wing and follows the
first shooter, again, driving to the middle using a jab step.
Each player shoots twice from each side.

The player's next move is from this same area. As before,
the player uses a jab step and drives toward the center of the
court. After dribbling twice, he should now take an extra step
forward with his inside foot, the one closest to the basket.
(This move done properly will result in the defensive man
continuing past the point where the offensive player will be
shooting from, giving him an open shot.) The player now pivots forward on the foot farthest from the basket, all the way
around, until he is square to the basket, and then shoots. The
key to this move is to stay low throughout the pivot, keeping
the ball in the shooting position, so that the player can release
the ball as soon as he is squared to the basket (Diagram 13-3).

The fourth station in this drill starts from the same spot as
the last two. The player again using a jab step drives to the
middle, but now reverses the ball using a spin dribble, and
continues to the basket for a lay-up. The player should be able
to execute this move in only three dribbles. It is important that
the player reverse pivot on his inside foot, pulling the ball
back with the same hand he is dribbling with (the hand fur-
thest from the basket), and make his last dribble in the lane. He
can then pick up the ball and go in for a lay-up (Diagram 13-4).
Each player should execute this move twice from each side.

The next shot starts from the same place. This time the
player uses a crossover step and drives to the corner, where he
squares to the basket and shoots. The ball is dribbled twice
with the outside hand, and as before, should come up hard to
the shooting hand on the second dribble. The players take two
shots from each side (Diagram 13-5).

The next move starts again from the wing area. Using a
crossover, the player again drives hard to the corner. As he
gets there, he now reverse pivots, using one more dribble, and
moves to a position where he can shoot the jump shot off the

backboard (Diagram 13-6). As before, it is important that the player square himself to the basket and take off and land in the same spot. We insist that the players shoot the ball off the backboard on this move.

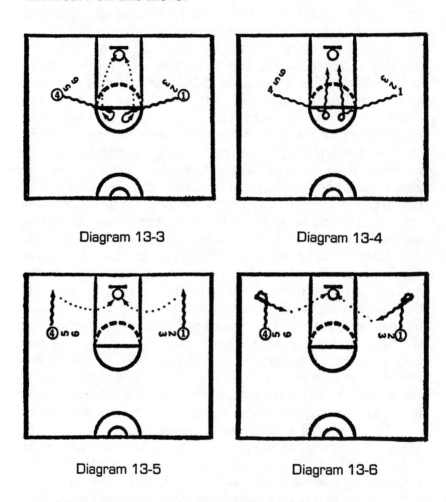

Diagram 13-3   Diagram 13-4

Diagram 13-5   Diagram 13-6

The last shot we use in this drill starts again from the wing. This time we want the offensive man to beat the defender in one dribble. Using a quick crossover move, the player puts the ball on the ground, picks it up, and floats to the basket. (We actually prefer that the player jump off of both feet at the same time, similar to the power lay-up move.) The player shoots the ball off the backboard on this move. He gets his own rebound, and continues to the other side. Each player shoots twice from each side, as they do throughout this drill (Diagram 13-7).

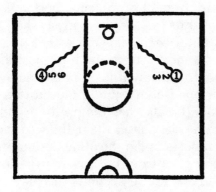

Diagram 13-7

Quick Shots. We run this drill with the players split up according to position. The posts are at one end, while the wings and point guards are at the other. We try to put three players at each basket, but will also run this drill with four at each. The posts will shoot from three inside positions. They start by posting up above the box with their backs to the basket. Another player is positioned on the wing with a basketball, while a third player is stationed out by the free throw line with a ball in his hands. As the coach blows the whistle, the player on the wing passes the ball to the post player. The post should call for the ball by showing which hand he wants the ball thrown to. (It's important that he alternates hands throughout the drill, to get used to catching the ball in either hand, and be able to make his moves going either way.) As the wing player passes the ball in, the player at the free throw line passes the ball to the player on the wing. The post must shoot until he scores. After he scores, he grabs the ball and passes it out to the player at the free throw line. The post then comes back to the box, calling for the ball. After 30 seconds, the coach blows the whistle and the players rotate positions: The wing goes to the post, the free throw line player goes to the wing, and the post player goes to the free throw line area. The players have five seconds to make the change, the coach blows the whistle and we start again. When all three players have had a chance to shoot from the post position we switch sides, running the drill from the opposite post area. Again, each player has 30 seconds to score as many baskets as he can, and then we rotate. After each player has shot from that position we have the posts move out to the high-post area. Starting at one corner of the free throw line, the post receives a pass from the player positioned above the circle on that side. He then pivots and shoots (he also has the option to drive to the basket). After he scores, he passes the ball out to the player he got it from, and then posts up on the other corner of the free throw circle receiving a pass from the player positioned above the circle on that side. After 30 seconds the players again rotate. The drill continues until all the players have had an opportunity to shoot from each spot. Diagram 13-8 shows what the drill looks like shooting from the low-post positions, while Diagram 13-9 shows how the drill will look from the high post. Each player must keep track of how many shots he makes (actually it works best if one of the nonshooters keeps track for the person shooting). At the end, we record the number of successful shots, and over the course of the season we chart each players progress. If you have enough personnel (assistant coaches and managers), it is preferred that you chart each shot as it is taken. This will aid the player in seeing where he has to make an adjustment on some of the various moves.

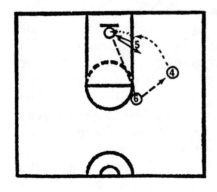

Diagram 13-8

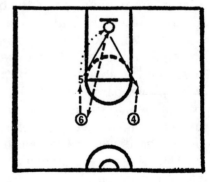

Diagram 13-9

The wings and points run the same drill but shoot from different spots on the floor. This time we start with the player who is going to shoot on the wing. A second player is positioned above the free throw circle. The third player is under the basket getting the rebound. The player on the wing begins to shoot as the whistle blows. After shooting, he takes two steps toward the baseline where he receives a pass from the player on the point. He should catch the ball in a shooting position and go up with it *immediately*. He then moves back to his original position where he receives another pass from the point. The rebounder always passes the ball out to the top. The shooter continues back and forth from the wing to the baseline for 30 seconds. At that time the players rotate, with the shooter going to the rebounding position, the passer going to the wing, and the rebounder going out to the point. When all the players have shot from the wing area, we have them switch sides. We now run the drill the same from the opposite side of the basket (Diagram 13-10).

When each of the players has shot from opposite sides of the basket, we move them out to the top of the free throw circle. We now have the other two players inside to rebound. As the player shoots he moves back and forth from one side of the circle to the other. After 30 seconds we rotate, and after everyone has shot, we record the total number of shots made. As with the posts, we chart the progress of each player throughout the season. Diagram 13-11 shows what this drill looks like when shooting from the top of the circle. We want

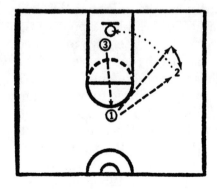

Diagram 13-10

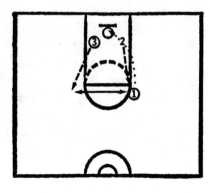

Diagram 13-11

the players to concentrate on three things in this drill. First, we want them to be able to catch the ball and be able to go right up with their shot. Second, we stress that they concentrate on the spot they are shooting at. (We prefer they pick out the ring—on the bottom of the rim—that is closest to them, or the backboard when using the glass.) Lastly, we want them to notice where they are missing their shots, (Is it off to the left or right, long or short?) and to recognize if there is a pattern (off to the left when they have moved left, etc.).

We also run both of these drills with the instruction that the players should use a pump fake either before or after they make their move or shoot. By getting the players to fake before they make their move or before they take their shot, it gives them practice in getting an opponent off balance and gives the shooter the added possibility of drawing the foul on his shot. We also instruct the players to use a fake and either a crossover move or a jab step before they shoot in the quick shot drill. We feel that shooting alone isn't enough, the players must also practice shooting off their moves and off a pump fake. It is possible to include this in the drill by alternating the drill every day using a different instruction before practice; that is, Monday—straight shooting, Tuesday—pump fake before move, Wednesday—pump fake before shot. You may also want to consider doing this drill more than once during a practice, changing the instruction before each drill.

2 on 2. We will play two-man basketball, varying our starting positions, depending on the aspect of the game we want to cover. The most common two-man game we concentrate on is between the wing and post. We will start the drill with the ball on the wing and an offensive player posting up above the box. Each man is covered by a defensive man. The wing has the option of starting the drill by either passing the ball into the post (reading the defender and offensive player's hand that's calling for the ball), or by dribbling to get a better passing angle, or driving past his man and going to the basket. Whenever he passes the ball into the post, the wing must cut either to the corner or to the free throw line; this prevents the defender from doubling down on the post. We continue to play until one team has scored three baskets. When the defensive team gets the ball they must bring it past the top of the circle. We then stop and have them start their offensive series from the wing (Diagram 13-12).

We can also run this drill starting from the point with a point guard and a wing or with a point guard and a post. In either case the person with the ball does not have to start the offense with a pass. However, we do discourage too much dribbling. Again, we use the rule that the dribble is to be used only to better the passing angle or to take the ball to the basket.

3 on 3. As in the "2 on 2" drill, we use a variety of combinations of players and starting positions. The most common combination we use is a point guard, a wing, and a post. The ball starts at the point with a backdoor cut by the wing. Once the play has begun we continue until one team has made three baskets. As before, when the defensive team gets the ball, they must first get the ball out to beyond the top of the circle before we stop. We then have them start their offensive series from there (Diagram 13-13).

The other combinations we will use in this drill are: a point and two wings, a wing and two posts, and a point guard and two posts.

4 on 4. We will run this the same as the "3 on 3" drill, using any combination of players, and starting from either the wing or the point. The main thing to be sure of here is that the players run the offense, with the appropriate reads and counters, and not just free-lance plays.

5 on 5. This is identical to "4 on 4" except that we always

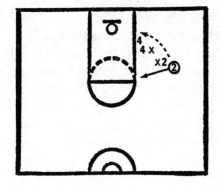

Diagram 13-12

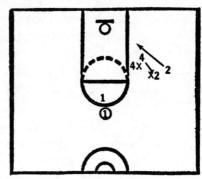

Diagram 13-13

start the ball on top, at the point guard position. Like the other drills, the defense must get the ball out to beyond the top of the free throw circle after gaining control of the ball.

Walk Through. In the beginning of the season, teach the offense by having the players walk through their cuts and options. At first, do this without a defense, and then after the players know what they are supposed to do, we will add a defense. As your team walks through the offense, tell the man with the ball to call out the options he is looking for along with the defensive reads he is supposed to make. This will make him more conscious of looking for these same options and reads when we pick up the tempo. After you have moved to the point of executing the offense comfortably against the defense, tell the players to jog through it, again calling out the options and reads available.

Reading the Defense. Break down the offense into the different areas that may arise in which the players will have to make the various reads of the defense. Instruct the defenders on what you want them to do and have the offensive players move through the appropriate counter to the defense. We will stress a number of different situations every day and run through each one at least ten times. After the players seem to have a feel for what you are trying to do, you may tell the defenders that you want them to make one of the various defensive adjustments, without letting the offensive player know what's about to happen. Obviously, you hope that the offensive player will react automatically, but if he doesn't, stop play and instruct him as to what he should have done. With practice and enough repetitions, most players get to the point where they will move to the right spot without much hesitation. It is important that you spend enough time on this area so that your players are familiar with the proper reads and counters, and make the right moves without having to think about them.

Pressure Work Up. We use all the drills mentioned here with the following added directive. We have the players on defense move up to offense only when they have been successful in accomplishing one of the following things: forcing a turnover, or making the offensive player take a bad shot or charge. The entire defensive team moves up to offense when they force a five-second count in the front court. The players who are waiting on the side to get into the drill can only take a defensive player's place when: The defender moves up to offense, the offensive player drives past the defender easily, the defender commits a reaching foul or fouls the shooter attempting to block his shot, the offensive man catches the ball in the lane or isn't contested as he cuts across the lane, or the defender doesn't rotate to help out on any penetrating pass or drive. When one of the above rules is broken, the player committing it moves out of the drill and to the end of line, and the next player moves up to take his place.

Percentage. When we run one of the drills involving shooting we specify that the players are to shoot a certain percentage during the drill. If they don't hit that percentage they must then run a sprint for each percentage point below the original number. We run this drill during our scrimmages as well. This makes the players aware of taking only good, high-percentage shots.

TEACHING THE BREAK

Long Outlet. This drill begins with a rebounder/outlet man in front of the basket and another player at the free throw line extended. The player in front of the basket throws the ball up off the glass to start the drill. At the same time the other player sprints out and touches the corner of the free throw line and then sprints downcourt toward the far basket. The player under the basket rebounds the ball and throws it downcourt to the release man, who catches it and tries to score. The rebound/outlet man on that end of the court steps in behind him and either rebounds the missed shot or takes the ball out of the net and sprints out-of-bounds, looking over his shoulder at the player from his side of the court who has released to the far end. The release player moves out to the corner of the free throw line and to the far end as soon as the player starts to shoot. (If the shot is missed, the rebounder does not run out of bounds to outlet, he passes the ball long right from there.) The drill continues with the outlet players moving to the end of the release line and vice-versa (Diagram 13-14). It is possible to run this drill with the player on the far end who is to be the next rebounder/outlet man to also act as a shot blocker as the player tries to shoot the lay-up. He is not to make contact with the shooter, just try to intimidate the release man or block the shot cleanly.

Outlet to the Point—Then Long. We run this drill much like the last drill except we start with a player on each side of the free throw line extended. As the ball is shot, the players sprint to the corners of the free throw line. The players talk to determine who will release and who will be the point guard. When they touch the corner of the free throw line, the release man heads for the far basket and the point steps to the side where the outlet man has the ball. The outlet man looks long for the release man and then passes the ball to the point guard. The point guard in turn pivots and throws the ball to the player who released (Diagram 13-15).

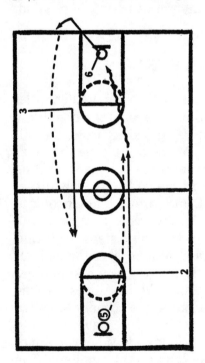

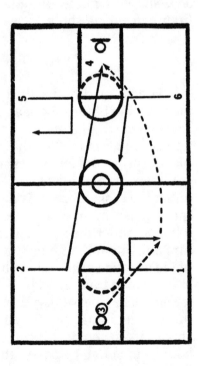

Diagram 13-14   Diagram 13-15

Point Outlet—Two-Man Break. This drill begins the same as the last one except that we tell the point guard to keep the ball as if the release man is not open. The player who released looks to see if the other wing is filling the third lane, and if he isn't, he steps to that side. The point guard now drives the ball up the court and to the basket. The rebounder on the far end plays these two players 2-on-1 (Diagram 13-16).

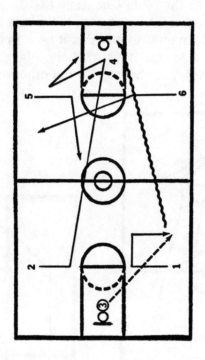

Diagram 13-16

Three-Man Break. We start with one player under the basket with the ball. There is a point guard at the top of the key, and a player at each corner of the free throw line. The player with the ball has the option of either throwing the ball off the glass and rebounding it (either side), or trying to make a basket and taking the ball out-of-bounds before he makes the outlet pass. As the ball is rebounded or taken out, the point guard moves to the outlet area on that side, the (2) man releases as soon as the ball is thrown up to the basket, and the (3) man holds until he sees what side the outlet pass is going to. The man who takes the ball out has the option of throwing it long to (2), to (1) on the same side he's on, or to the opposite side to (3). If the ball is thrown long, (2) must try to score and (1) and (3) trail in case he misses. If the ball is thrown to (1), he must turn and look long to (2), and then take the ball up on the dribble (Diagram 13-17). If the ball is thrown crosscourt to (3), (1) must move to that side (Diagram 13-18). The players stay down on that side of the court until the whole team has run the drill. We then turn around and run it back to the other side of the court. It is also important that the player who made the initial outlet pass trail the play to the other end.

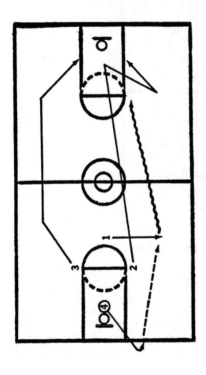

Diagram 13-17

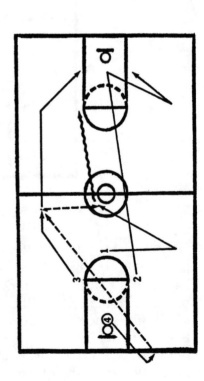

Diagram 13-18

Five-Man Break. Walk through the break the first few times to make sure everyone understands their role, then pick up the pace, going a little faster each time, until you are able to run it at top speed, but still under control.

Continuous Break. This drill is simply the break run without a defense. However, tell the players to run it a certain number of times in a row. The same unit will then run it the designated number of times before the next group jumps in to take their place. Allow only two shots each time down the floor. If they don't score within those two, they react as if they were on defense and break to the far end. If a shot is made we now take the ball quickly out-of-bounds and run the break from there.

Designated Shooter. Run the break, again without a defense, but designate what option we want the players to look for. One time, tell your players to look to the release man and throw him the ball, and the next time tell them to hit the wing in the far lane, or the first trailer coming down the lane.

Break vs. Defense. There are a number of variations that can be run with this drill. First, run this drill with the team you want to run the break on *defense.* As the other players try to score, this team will try to get the ball and break from either a steal, rebound, or from a basket. As soon as the ball changes hands, begin the break with the team that was on offense getting back to defend the break. Another way we will run this drill is with a designated number of defensive players back to start. Put either one, two, or three defensive men under the basket that you will be running the break toward. The remaining players will stay at the far end to begin and shoot the ball to start the break. This will give us a number of different looks that the players will have to adjust to as they move the ball up the court.

Five-Man into the Offense. This is similar to the "Five-Man Break," except you want the players to *not* shoot, and to continue right into the offense. We will also tell the offense that they must make a certain number of passes before anyone can shoot. Along with this we will designate how many times the ball must go into the post before they can shoot. By forcing the team to make a certain number of passes it will do two things: (1) It forces them to run through the offense, and (2) it forces them to be patient. This also works against a defense. This drill will make the team aware of the fact that a better shot will usually open up for someone if they are patient and do not rush.

11-Man Fastbreak. This drill starts with the players aligned as in Diagram 13-19. The ball is in the hands of the player in the center of the court. He starts the drill by dribbling the ball toward one of the baskets. The other two players at half court with him break down their lanes and go to the basket. The player with the ball drives to the corner of the free throw line. The two defensive players at that end play in tandem (one behind the other). The offensive players shoot until they score or the defense steals the ball or gets a rebound. As the players are playing at that end, the next two players [(6) and (7)] step out onto the court near the top of the free throw circle. They have determined between themselves who is going to be the point guard and who is going to be the release

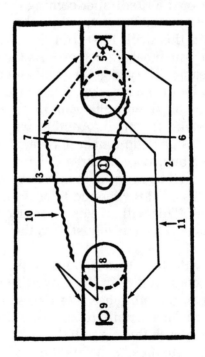

Diagram 13-19

man. As the defense gets the ball, start to break to the other end. The rebounder turns and looks downcourt to the release man, then to the point guard who has moved to the same side of the rebound. (If the shot is made, the defensive team takes the ball out-of-bounds to start the break.) The point guard then drives the ball up the court, and the release man breaks out to the wing area, after checking to make sure the other wing has gotten out on the break. The other lane is filled by the player who did not outlet the ball to start the break. These three players now go 3-on-2 against players (8) and (9) at the other end of the court. When the ball changes hands, we break to the other end again. This continues for either a designated time or number of baskets.

Coaching Point: The players must step onto the court and get ready to break as soon as the ball passes them near half court, and the easiest rotation is to have the player who shot and the outlet man go to the end of the lane lines, while the two offensive players who did not shoot stay in the lane and play defense the next time the ball comes down the court (Diagram 13-19).

TEACHING THE PRESS OFFENSE

Walk Through. Have the players walk through the press offense primarily when they have to execute it from the set position. At the same time, teach them the various options they have (point and wing or third man in line exchanging responsibilities). After the players have walked through it and feel comfortable with the press offense, step up the pace and have them go through it half- and three-quarter speed, and finally have them go through it full speed, making sure they practice each option a number of times in the process.

The Press Offense vs. the Press. Once the players have mastered the pattern of the press offense, the best way to practice it is to go against all the different presses your team will encounter throughout the year. The most common full-court presses are: the man-to-man, the man-to-man jump switch, the 1–2–1–1 (1–2–2) zone press, and the 2–2–1 zone press. One of the things you may want to emphasize is that the players should execute the offense as diagrammed. To vary from the offense will only lead to confusion and turnovers. Stress that if all of the players are in their proper areas, someone is bound to be open.

As we mentioned earlier, in most of our 2-on-2, 3-on-3, and 4-on-4 drills, the offense must get the ball out beyond the top of the key before they can start their offensive series. We feel this conditions them in two ways: First, they are always looking to run the break, and second, they must get the ball in against some kind of pressure.

TEACHING TEMPO

Situations. This drill is run two different ways. When teaching the players what you want them to do, set up specific situations and practice the various techniques you want them to perfect. For example, tell your players you want them to take time off the clock. We then have them practice running that aspect of the Multiflex Offense against a defense (this of course, is after they have learned what you want them to do). Practice all the different situations you anticipate that you may possibly come up against over the course of a season. When the players make a mistake, stop the drill and start over until they have gotten to the stage where they are quite proficient in that aspect of the game.

The second way to run this drill is to have the players draw from a pack of situation cards. The different cards will have the score of the game, the time remaining, the number of time-outs left for both teams, and what both teams want to do. As the drill goes on, the situation may change and we will give different directions for each of the situations that may arise. Each card will vary; sometimes the first unit will be down by a good number of points with only a few minutes remaining, and other times they will be up by six or eight with just a minute or so left in the game. This drill can be quite fun and educational, provided that you have cards to cover the different situations that are possible in the last 2 to 8 minutes of a game. For best results the drill should be run as close as possible to game conditions. You may also find it helpful to remove the card that was picked until all the different situations have been explored. You can then put all the cards together again and start over. By practicing this you will accomplish two main goals. First, the players will know what you expect them to do in a given situation, and second, because they will have already practiced it, the players will feel more comfortable and confident when they are called upon to execute in that same situation in a game.

These are just a few of the drills that may be run. Most of the other drills are the same ones everyone else runs in the course of the season. These were mentioned here because they are somewhat different from the drills typically run by most coaches, and they incorporate specific aspects of the offense in the drills that will teach the different aspects of the offense to the players.

Index